WHODUNIT
PUZZLES

WHODUNIT
PUZZLES

MYSTERIES FOR THE
SUPER SLEUTH
TO SOLVE

Tim Dedopulos

This edition published in 2022 by Arcturus Publishing Limited
26/27 Bickels Yard, 151–153 Bermondsey Street,
London SE1 3HA

AD008552NT

Printed in the US

CONTENTS

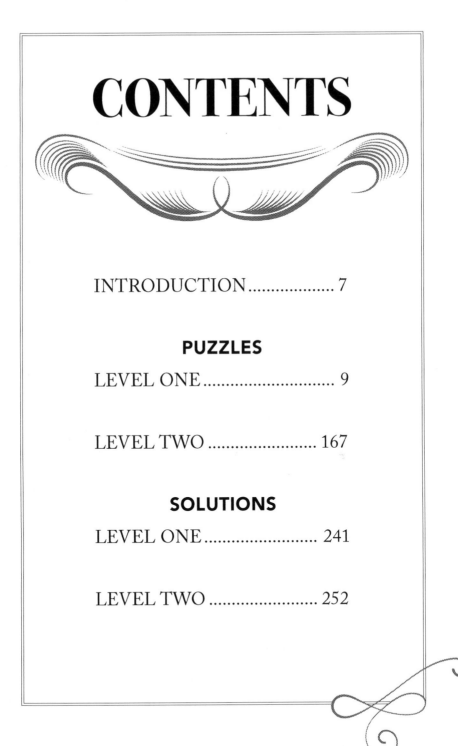

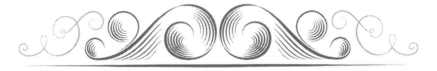

INTRODUCTION

Solving puzzles is an almost universally beloved pastime, allowing us some time to switch off from our worries and cares and giving us the chance to exercise our brains. Tackling the conundrums presented here will prove just as entertaining. Each of these whodunit puzzles contains everything you need to solve the mystery and identify the culprit on the page… all you have to do is spot the omission, falsehood, or incongruity that gives the game away.

Miss Mary Miller

Inspector "Paddington" Parnacki

The puzzles in Level 1 are shorter and more straightforward; those in Level 2 comprise longer narratives, include more characters and complications to pick

Mrs. Warren

your way through and may be a little trickier to solve. Plus, there are some red herrings to throw you off the scent!

Helping you in your task are three inimitable detectives—you will follow each in turn as they guide you through the scene, evidence, and suspects—Inspector Ignatius "Paddington" Parnacki, Miss Mary Miller, and Mrs. Emma Warren. Should you need further assistance, at least one hint is provided at the end of each puzzle. If more than one hint is offered, try to read only one at a time, returning to read the next if you're still stuck—and if all else fails, the solutions can be found at the back.

So, without further ado, go forth, and happy sleuthing!

LEVEL ONE

PUZZLES

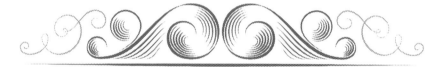

THE TAILOR

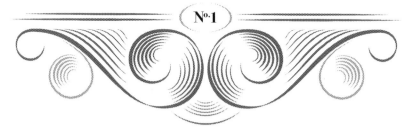

A lbert Giles had been thirty-eight at the time of his death, and had been making his way home on an otherwise unremarkable Tuesday afternoon. A tall man of average build, his sallow skin and thinning hair were in distinct contrast to the elegant cut of his clothing. He'd been stabbed in the neck, a savage and unpleasant wound, but at least death had been mercifully swift. The general level of disarray suggested that the man had been quickly searched for valuables, and no wallet, watch, or trinkets had been found with him.

The report noted that the victim had been a tailor for a large clothing manufacturer, but his corpse evidenced a notable lack of the fastidiousness common in members of that profession. His body had been found slumped in a street-side doorway moments after death, and showed plenty of blood and street dirt. A pair of gore-marked leather work-gloves and a short, broad dagger were found with him. But Mr. Giles was also liberally sprinkled with patches of soft, dusty

fluff of an uncommon shade of powder-blue, including in his hair and eyebrows. The lack of any similar deposits at the murder site strongly suggested he had acquired this coating at his workplace. Grass-tinged threads speckled his shirt and jacket, and the front of his trousers was covered with little burrs of lint in cornflower blue, black, cream, and beige.

Inspector Parnacki set the report aside, and brushed an errant speck off his sleeve. Officers had apprehended several men in the near vicinity of the murder, and they now awaited questioning. Whether any one of them was a viable suspect had yet to be ascertained. The discarded gloves were larger than the hands of all three men, and none of them showed any blood spatters or possessed any of the dead man's valuables.

The first of the detainees, Ray Hollingsworth, was in his late twenties. Five feet six in height, he was muscular with a heavy jaw and beetling brows, and wore thick, simply made work clothes of a muddy hue. When he spoke, his voice was rough from years of misuse. He made little effort to disguise his impatience with the proceedings. "Yeah, I heard there was some poor bugger copped it. I don't know nothing about it. Didn't hear nothing, didn't see nothing, never heard of the bloke. Yes, I walk through the area every night. I work down on the Blanchard dock, and home is past St. Joseph's. Look, I'm not going to deny that me and the lads get a bit tasty sometimes on a Friday night, but I've never killed anyone, not even that sod that came swinging at me with a bill-hook couple of years back. Stevedore is an honest profession, and I'm an honest man. I don't need to be going around robbing and killing and carrying on."

Daniel Hanson was several years younger than Hollingsworth. He had a mop of dark, curly hair, and unusually bright blue eyes. He was wearing an ugly, shapeless homespun suit and a tattered green muslin shirt, and he clutched a cap in his hands. A grubby red neckerchief did a poor job of hiding the pockmarks scattered around his neck. His voice held traces of a habitual wheedling whine. "I'm a rag and bone man, me. Work with my uncle, Roddy. That's what I was about, see? Of an evening, he drops me in a particular locality, and I have a little look around, see if there's anything dumped in the area what's worth salvaging. In the morning, we come back round and if no one wants it, we cart it off. You don't get far in the trade just sticking to your regular round, not nowadays. Now you mention it, I did hear someone shout out, but it wasn't none of my business so I didn't pay it no mind. That's really the only thing I can tell you, and that's a fact."

The third man, Alan Gordon, was a little older than the others, somewhere in his thirties. He had short reddish-brown hair and a tidy moustache, and the overall impression he gave was of profound fatigue. Even his smooth, cheap off-white suit and pale shirt looked tired. His eyes darted around the room constantly, and his voice was thin and nervous. "I don't know that I can be much use to you, Inspector Parnacki. I'm sorry. I start work at five in the morning—I'm a clerk at Petersons—and by the time the day is done, I'm rather hard-used. Mr. Peterson is, ah, keenly involved in proceedings at the office. My wife and I have three little ones under the age of two, so my nights are not restful. By the time I'm heading home of an evening, the world is something of a blur. I have a vague recollection of running feet before the whistles started, but I'm far from confident even of that. Well, no, it's not easy managing on my salary, but my wife takes in some washing, and we get by. It'll get easier when my eldest can start bringing a little home in a year or two. Until then, we endure."

After the interviews, Parnacki tracked down his sergeant. "I believe I have somewhere to start, Sullivan. Let the other two loose, but make sure you have their home and work addresses."

Who is Parnacki suspicious of, and why?

HINT:

Detritus.

REBECCA

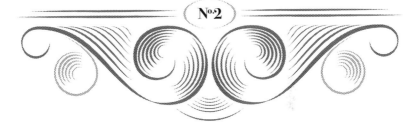

№·2

A ylward House looked oddly forlorn in the pale February
light, with all its windows and doors buttoned up tight
against the cold, and the ivy wrapped close around it like
a shawl. It had been a month since the untimely death of its last
resident, Rebecca Thomas, but the only signs of disorder were the
branches and other bits of wind-fall littering the sweeping lawns.
Mary Miller looked across the statue garden to the copse nearby, and
sighed heavily.

Beside her, Ruth Derry nodded, her movement somewhat
hampered by the big coat she was bundled up in. "It's a strange and
terrible business, Mary."

"Thirty-two is far too young. No age at all."

"There's no sense to it. She had a rocky time for a while, but she
got over Michael's loss four years ago. In fact, she told me just after
the new year that she was courting again, a rather dashing banker
that she met through the Jameses. That Beatty fellow who'd taken a

fancy to her was put out, but everybody else thought it was a great development." Ruth paused, her face concerned. "Not that she'd been lonely, you understand. I was far from her only friend, and on the occasions when she declined company, it was only so that she could lose herself in some book or other. What possible reason could there have been to drive her to leap from a damned window like that?"

"Were there any financial worries?"

"Lord, no. Poor Michael left her perfectly comfortable."

Miss Miller took a moment to gather her words cautiously. "Not all sadness is visible, Ruth. Even to those we love. Some people bear very heavy burdens in the deepest secrecy, unable to let them show."

"Well, yes, I do know, the poor devils." She shook her head. "But that really wasn't Rebecca. Perhaps she put on a brave face for the public, but after Michael's heart attack, she made no efforts to hide her misery from me. I spent many long evenings with her, keeping her company in her desolation. She never flinched from honest expression of her grief, or any other dark feeling for that matter. She'd been through a hard journey, but she was still the girl I knew at school—lively, curious, and engaging. A little wiser perhaps, but there was no abyss within her spirit. Nobody can understand it."

"Did the police investigate at all?"

"Oh, they sent a couple of men around. Her maid had been in the village with her parents that night, so it was the housekeeper who found her on her way in, early the next morning. It wasn't immediately obvious what had happened, so the woman called for assistance. The officers told her and the maid to ensure nothing was touched anywhere, and then made a thorough survey. There were no signs of any missing items or valuables, and with a short, sad note on the bedroom dresser, the matter was swiftly dealt with." She waved a sweeping hand at the house, grief twisting at her expression. "The maid couldn't bring herself to go back inside. She thought maybe if she'd been there... Poor girl. Anyway, Aylward is exactly as Rebecca left it, and I dare say it'll stay that way until her brother finds the heart to do something about it."

Miss Miller's eyes tightened. "Exactly, Ruth?"

The other woman nodded.

"You're certain?"

"Mary? Whatever is it? You're scaring me a little. Yes. I'm quite certain. The police were most insistent."

Fighting to keep the rising fury from her face, Miss Miller crossed her arms tightly. "We need to go immediately to the authorities, Ruth. Rebecca could not have taken her own life."

Why does Miss Miller think the woman was murdered?

HINT:

House.

INTRODUCING MRS. WARREN

№.3

Emma Warren inspected herself as best as she could in the small mirror above the sink. She carefully straightened one lapel, and adjusted her skirts so that the seam fell square off the hip. Still not quite right. She relaxed her shoulders, slouched a little, tried to think defeated thoughts. Finally satisfied, she left the room to blend in with the real cleaners of The Carson Hotel.

She lined up among the other women, her expression carefully off-putting. She needn't have bothered. No one was talking. If any of the staff were friends, they kept it well hidden under a patina of exhaustion and low-grade fear. A disinterested shift supervisor passed on her assignment in a bored tone, a section of corridor that included the target room. Grabbing a cart of supplies and a stack of fresh laundry, Emma headed off to her do her job.

Fitting in meant doing the work systematically, like anyone else would. It wasn't fun, but in what world did anyone imagine cleaning hotel rooms to be anything other than drudgery? After four rooms, she finally came to 313. Like the others, it was expensively appointed and beneath the dirt and chaos of uncaring occupancy, it looked nice enough to justify the room rate. More or less.

After so many identical spaces, the missing lamp stood out like an absent tooth. There had been no guest in the room that day, no cleaning slated. Evening inspection had discovered the lamp shattered, but there should have been no entry. It was a good place to start. She looked around the space where the lamp should have been. Under the table, almost hidden by the swirling weaves of the carpet, there was a

small bronze air grille dabbed with little smears of rust. Reaching down, she hooked a nail around one bar and tugged. It rattled, loose enough to be almost falling off. She filed it away in one corner of her mind, and got on with her work.

Six hours after they'd started, she and the other cleaners were given their allotted fifteen minutes to relieve themselves and consume such luncheons as they'd brought with them.

The floors had staggered break-times, so the hotel only needed to provide room for a few women at one time. No one was particularly interested in wasting time talking, but Emma introduced herself wearily, and the others reciprocated in kind. The aging woman, bent-backed and sour, was Elizabeth. The smiler was Valeria, and her accent marked her as foreign. Meagan had a scabbed knuckle and hints of poorly removed eye-shadow that she'd been lucky to get away with. Sybil, sallow and wilting, looked scarcely fit enough to cope. Betsy had challenging eyes, and clearly little love for newcomers. The last girl, sullen and resentful, just grunted. That would be Frances, then. Emma dropped her eyes back to her sandwich, and resumed eating.

That night, dressed to the nines and so made up that even her mother would barely have recognized her, Emma went back to The Carson, and up to the manager's office.

Mr. McGill looked pleased to see her. "Mrs. Warren. Any progress?"

"Yes, sir," Emma replied. "I have a solid idea of where the lamp fits in, and who your thief is. My boss will book in tomorrow, with a prize too tempting to pass up and an itinerary with a clear hole in. Hold 313 empty, and put me—or a security man, if you prefer—in the closet in there. We'll have her dead to rights."

Who does Emma suspect of being the thief?

HINT:

Grille.

THE THROTTLED CLERK

Inspector Parnacki rapped sharply on the front door of the Winton house. It was a pleasant-looking dwelling, tidy and well maintained. It spoke of comfortable middle-class respectability, as befitted the home of a bank clerk. Sergeant Patricks fidgeted beside him, clearly bored, but a frown was enough to get the man to subside.

There were some steps from inside, and then the door opened. A sad, tired little man opened the door. He was unkempt, and somewhat distracted. The fellow looked up and blinked owlishly once or twice.

"I am Inspector Parnacki. This is the house of Mr. David Winton?"

"Yes, of course. Thank you for coming so swiftly, Inspector. I'm Tom Leslie, Rhoda's brother. Um. Dave's brother-in-law. Please, come in. Nobody has touched D . . . anything. Rhoda couldn't stay in the house, not with... Well. She's round mine at the moment, with Hannah. That's my wife. She asked me to tell you that she'll be happy to answer

"Her people?" Miss Miller asked, deliberately keeping her voice light.

"Absolutely," Kitty muttered. "And say what you like, I don't trust that girl. I've made no secret of it. Now you have to be shot of her, and that'll be the end of it."

"If you're certain..." Maureen's reluctance was clear. "I suppose I'll have to speak to Parrish."

"You do that and we'll all be happier." Kitty grimaced. "Now be a dear and tell me what that cook of yours is doing for lunch today."

Norrie brightened. "Pottage, served with new potatoes and a barley loaf. We have our guest to thank for that, I think. Your visits always bring out the best in her, Miss Miller."

Kitty looked over at Miss Miller, and harrumphed. "That's one ray of light, I suppose."

Miss Miller rose to her feet. "Maureen my dear, I forgot that I brought along a fascinating study of a lark to show you. I left it in the drawing room. Ladies, if you'd excuse us?" She helped her friend to her feet, and bustled her out of the room.

Maureen allowed herself to be escorted a short distance away, and then stopped. "Mary, you've got that look in your eye. What is it?"

Miss Miller patted Maureen's hand. "I don't think your aunt is being entirely honest with Norrie or you, I'm afraid."

Why doesn't Miss Miller believe Maureen's aunt?

HINT:

Visit.

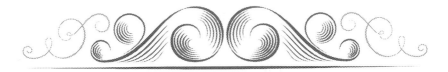

THE HARKAWAY

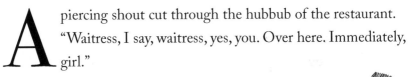

A piercing shout cut through the hubbub of the restaurant. "Waitress, I say, waitress, yes, you. Over here. Immediately, girl."

Emma Warren put the dirty plates she was carrying onto an empty table, and made her way over to the window. The woman at the table was in her late thirties, with fading brown hair and an overweening sense of self-satisfaction. She'd been relentlessly unpleasant all luncheon, and seemed determined to finish on a high note.

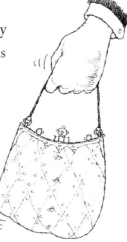

Dropping her head, Emma put on a simpering smile. "Yes, madam?"

The woman glared at her, and pushed a deeply browned apple core around her dessert plate. "I demand to see the manager this instant. Some scallywag has made off with my purse. I won't have it, do you hear?"

Well. Maybe a degree of unpleasantness was justified. "Of course, madam. I'll fetch him this instant."

She left the indignant customer, and hurried back to the small office off the kitchen. The manager was a thin man, and clearly suffering from the stress of recent events. She knocked on his door, and gave him a sympathetic look. "There's been another one, Mr. Ragland."

The manager winced. "I see."

"The customer wants to see you."

"Of course they do." He stood, rubbing at his temple. "You'd better take me to..."

"Her," Emma said. "I don't know her name yet."

Ragland nodded glumly, and followed Emma back to the window table. She left him to introduce himself, and went out to the coat check. The young man who staffed it looked up as she approached.

"You been keeping your list sharp today, Hal?" she asked.

He nodded. "Of course, Mrs. Warne. Everyone in and out, by the clock."

"I'm going to need the book. Do you have some other paper to keep track with for a bit?"

"Yes, Mrs. Warne." He held out the book he'd been tracking entries with.

She took it, and gave him a smile. "Good work, Hal. Keep it up."

When she got back to the window table, the customer was busily haranguing Mr. Ragland about the quality of his staff and the criminal filth at large in the world today and all the usual nonsense. He glanced over at Emma, saw the book in her hands, and nodded. As soon as the

woman paused to draw a breath, he steeled himself and leapt in. "May I ask when the theft occurred, madam?"

"Well just now, obviously! I found the purse gone, and called your dozy girl over, and—"

"Forgive me," Ragland said quickly, "but were you actually at the table when it happened?"

"Of course not! *I'm* not half-asleep. I finished with my indifferent cheese and nipped to the powder room. I can't have been more than two minutes. When I returned, it was gone."

Emma glanced at the list that Hal had been keeping. In the previous five minutes, no people had gone in or out. She looked at Ragland, and shook her head.

"I see," the manager said unhappily. "I'm very sorry, and I apologize if you found your dessert dissatisfactory."

"So you should be," the woman snapped. "The cheddar was very bland, the crackers were far too hard, and I'm astonished any modern establishment would expect a guest to slice her own pieces of apple. The good Lord knows I'm not one to make a fuss, but I was of a mind to complain even before I was robbed blind."

She continued on ranting, but Emma tuned her out. There weren't any staff waiting this lunchtime, so she'd seen to everyone. The session was winding down, and almost all of the other tables had paid up and cleared out over the last half-hour. An old couple down the other end of the room were having a high old time listening in, and good for them, but they didn't make for plausible thieves. So where the devil had the woman's purse gone?

Then a thought hit her, and she pulled the manager away from the astonished woman's table with a cursory apology.

"Our angry lady isn't telling you the truth about her bathroom visit," she told him.

Why does Emma think the woman is lying about her visit to the bathroom?

HINT:

Dessert.

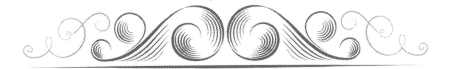

BISHOP

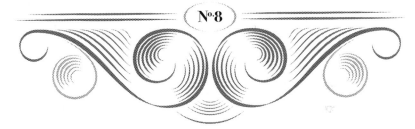

N°8

Walter Betteridge died in his office, on a Thursday evening. An importer of goods from the continent, he had been in his fifties. Cause of death had been a very heavy blow to the back of his neck when he fell back onto the protruding corner of a heavy marble shelf in his office, but he had also suffered a sprained ankle, a radiating fracture on the underside of his forearm, and a heavily bruised jaw. For once, the identity of his killer was already known—his business partner, Ian Bishop, who insisted he had been simply defending himself.

Inspector Parnacki met Bishop in the company's premises to go through the man's story. Betteridge

and Bishop had separate offices off the company's main suite, both very similar.

"This was Walt's room," Bishop said. "We were due for a quick meeting after the staff had gone home, to discuss an issue we were having with some cured Danish meats. That may sound dry, but it's actually been weighing on us heavily for the last few weeks. A lot of our money is tied up in that shipment, and the supplier is proving worryingly difficult to get hold of. I made that particular deal, but I had no clue that Walt was blaming me for the state of affairs."

"He was angry with you?" Parnacki asked.

Bishop sighed. "I didn't think so. I still can't believe it. But we were talking and he just snapped. He went mad, like he was a completely different person suddenly, or a rabid wolf, or something. He snatched up the poker from the fireplace, snarling and spitting. I fell back, but he sprang at me, and swung the damned thing at my head! I managed to sway out of the way, and the old boxing instincts took over. I snapped a punch at him, and caught him square." The man tapped a spot on his jaw-line. "He dropped the poker—that's it there, I haven't moved it—and stumbled back. There was nothing for him to steady himself on. He tripped on the rug, and fell back onto the shelf with a horrible crunch. After that, he just collapsed like a discarded marionette. It was horrible. It *is* horrible. The whole thing was over so quickly, yet it was so utterly catastrophic."

"What happens to his share of the company?"

"It passes to his wife, Ella. But given the state we're in right now, I don't know if we can continue trading. I could have dealt with writing off the Danish deal if Walt were here, but without him, I don't know that I have the heart to salvage it. Perhaps Herr Nilaus will still come through, and we can stay in business. But it's unlikely. If it doesn't happen, it's better to shut up shop now, before we incur further liabilities. Kinder on Ella, too. Six months of pressing on pluckily could easily see us deep into debts, and I'd much rather spare her the risk of having to find money to wind up the business. It's going to be hard enough for her without Walt as it is. It doesn't seem fair to risk making things tougher."

"It certainly doesn't," Parnacki said. "Ian Bishop, you are under arrest for the murder of Walter Betteridge."

Why does Parnacki think Bishop deliberately murdered Walter?

HINT:

Fracas.

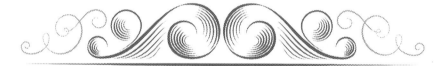

PANHURST

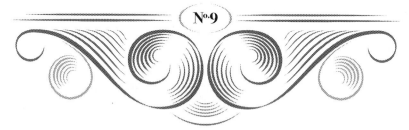

Nº.9

"You just don't expect it in a village like Panhurst." Ania Bailey swept her arm out in a wide arc, narrowly missing a small and rather ugly vase on the side-table next to her. "I suppose that's naïve of me. But we all know each other, and have done for donkey's years. It gives you a sense of safety." She sighed bitterly. "A false one, as it transpires."

Miss Miller nodded sympathetically. "You mentioned an heirloom?"

"That's the worst part of it. If he'd filched the silverware, like any normal thief, I wouldn't have minded as much. But he beelined for my great-grandmother's medicine chest, damn his eyes. It's an 1820 model, teak box lined in azure velvet, with decorated crystal bottles which had caps inlaid with very fine gold filigree. None of the little compartment draws were damaged. It was complete, too. It still had all four pairs of scissors, and even that odd tiny hook thing. Do you know how rare it is to find a George III memorial medicine chest that still has all its original bits and pieces?"

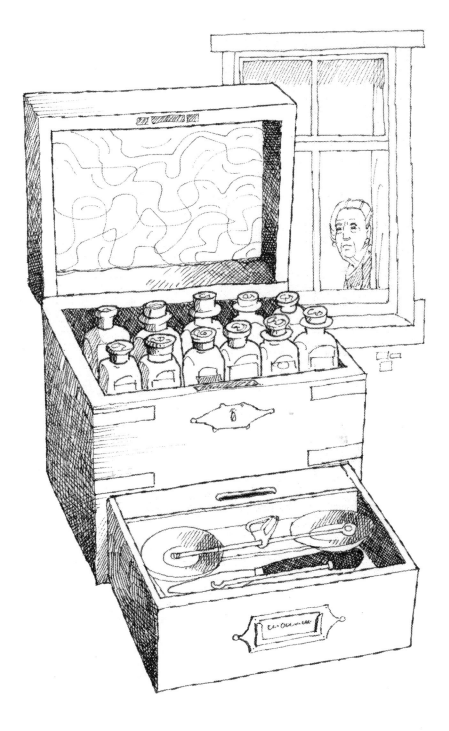

"As hen's teeth."

"Exactly, yes. It's not the value I object to. I'd never have sold it, and I'd never dream of replacing it, so the price is moot. Except as motive to steal it, of course. Damn good eye he must have had, that lad. I suppose it comes with the territory."

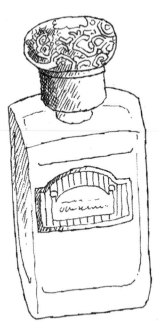

"Less so than you'd think," Miss Miller said. "Most burglars are far from expert, and they shy away from easily identifiable stuff mostly. They want the things that will fetch a quick, easy price, ideally ones that are tough to trace to any specific victim. They're much simpler to sell on, you see."

Ania gave her a very odd look. "I suppose that makes sense. It doesn't exactly help, though, Mary. It makes me even unluckier than I thought. I had to get the only thief around with a nose for Georgian antiquities."

"It's curious, that's for sure. What do the police think?"

"Oh, they're cautiously optimistic of course, all very polite, but you can tell they don't think they'll catch the boy."

Miss Miller arched an eyebrow. "You keep referring to him as young. Did you see him?"

"Lord above, no. I didn't miss him by much, though. I'd been out on the marshes all afternoon on the other side of the drift. So many birds that'd never be seen dead there for the rest of the year. Fascinating. Anyway, I've got one of those flashlight things—a wonderful idea, they are, I never go out without mine now—so it's no problem making my way back to the house after dark, even on a Stygian night like that. As the sun set, I made my way to The Green Feather for a cup of tea and a spot of cake as usual. I got home an hour or so later, at about six thirty. It was Mrs. Colfer who saw him. She lives two doors down, on the other side of the road."

"Oh?"

"Yes. She's almost always there by her window, knitting away and twitching the curtains. Knows everyone's business. Useful this time, though. A young man it was, tall and skinny with hair like a mop-head. Dark trousers, deep blue shirt, light boots, and a leather pack on his shoulder. As she tells it, he stalked down the road from the direction of Coreham, avoiding any hint of illumination. He went straight past her house, and up my garden path. He was back out a couple of minutes later, and returned the way he'd come. Ten past six, by the clock on her wall."

"Ania dear, I'm afraid that's absolute nonsense."

"Whatever do you mean?"

Miss Miller shook her head. "Your Mrs. Colfer is lying like a sailor."

Why does Miss Miller think Mrs. Colfer is lying?

HINT:

Timing.

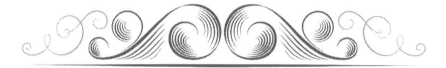

PERGAMUM

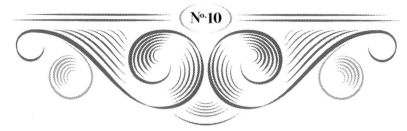

A ugustus Manby had not been popular with anyone very much. Respected, perhaps, for the cut-throat success of his shipping operation, Pergamum, but without any hint of personal fondness. When Inspector Parnacki had informed his wife of his murder, she'd reacted with suspicion, followed shortly by agonized, tear-streaked laughter. That had been more sympathy than the rest of his family had evidenced. He'd been feared by his staff, and if he'd had personal friends, they were well hidden, and unmentioned in calendar or diary. The gentlemen's club he frequented was famed for its asocial charter, and members were required to maintain quiet solitude.

Manby had been found in his office, cut and stabbed more than sixty times. A muscular six-foot forty-four-year-old with a bull-neck and massive shoulders, he certainly appeared to have put up an impressive fight. His office was almost completely wrecked, with one visitor's chair smashed to pieces and another missing one arm and leg, several splintered picture frames, and a pine bookcase that had been

utterly destroyed. The main office chair and desk had fared best, the desk merely upended, and the chair still in place behind where it would have sat, with just a neat slice through it high up on the back. Several cabinets of files had been thrown over, and the remnants of papers and books littered the room calf-deep. Blood splattered over everything.

The corpse had been found in the middle of all the destruction, sliced and diced repeatedly, with wounds on all sides and from multiple angles. Many of them were reasonably superficial, which certainly fitted with a brawl. The murder weapon, a stiletto dagger, was left piercing through one eye and into the brain. Despite this last desecration, the autopsy had found the cause of death to be a deep stab past the spine into the heart, the placement of the dagger a statement rather than a finishing blow. Time of death was thought to be around 11 pm, a not-uncommon time for the victim to be still at work.

According to numerous sources, Manby had been openly contemptuous of those he considered his lessers—almost everyone, it seemed. At his very best, he was curt and impatient, but fits of rage could come across him at the drop of a pin, and provoke the most extraordinary tirades.

Manby's son, Langley, was a junior clerk with the family business. He was slight and shy, and seemed to constantly anticipate a surprise beating. "Father didn't have enemies. An enemy suggests ongoing rivalry, a person who opposes one's will repeatedly. Father only had victims. That was true in his business, in his personal life, and, I'm afraid, in his family life. There were a great many people who never wished Father dead, but I can tell you categorically that not a one of them had ever met him in person. He was an affliction that I suffered from, and it is difficult to imagine what life might mean beyond that. I think I might become a florist. That sounds incredible."

His assistant, a slim man named Reginald Payne, suggested that the man's success in business had been achieved mostly through personal ferocity and the absolute denial of any fact he took issue with. "Windbag—I can call him that openly, at last—was, frankly, the most atrocious bully you can imagine. He got started in the trade by terrorizing his bank manager into a dubious loan at advantageous rates, and never looked back from there. My only surprise is that it took this long for someone to off the horrible bugger." Payne smoothed down his tidy hair compulsively, and suppressed a shudder. "From the look of it, he put up one hell of a fight. You'll be looking for a six-and-a-half-foot navvy he was barely aware of double-crossing, I wager."

"No," Parnacki said, eyeing him. "The murderer was someone that the victim knew well enough to discount as a threat, likely someone lacking in significant physical strength."

Why does Parnacki think the murderer was well known to the victim?

HINT:

Office.

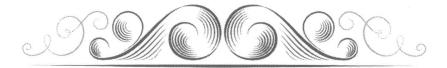

STAR HOUSE

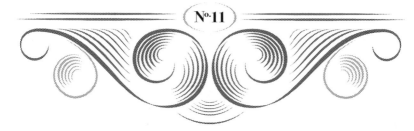

O swald Ware was an enthusiastic member of the Ornithological Society with a particular interest in the flight habits of geese. His first cousin Leona Whitten lived on the north side of the city, and her home, Star House, occupied much of the top of Star Hill. It was a very pleasant estate, with wonderful views both down onto the city and out over the northern woodlands and fields. A smallish lake at the foot of the hill on the north side was

a very popular spot with both birds and their admirers. So three or four times a year, Oswald imposed upon his cousin's hospitality and hosted members of the Society at Star House for a day of ornithology and sandwiches.

Miss Miller had been a regular attendee at the Star House Bird Days for a decade, and over the years had come to know Leona rather well. She was a pleasant woman with a lively intellect. Her primary fascination was with bone china, and she was more comfortable at home with a book than out at some social event, which made her a very interesting conversationalist. On Bird Day visits, Miss Miller typically planned to spend the morning with the Society, and when they all went back out after lunch, to remain behind to catch up with her friend.

For once, however, Leona was deeply out of sorts. "Some rotter pinched Sir Percival," she finally admitted, her voice glum.

"The gilded blue parrot?"

"That's the one. He's a genuine Spode from 1799, and very finely decorated."

Miss Miller frowned. "It wasn't one of us, was it?"

"He was there this morning," she said. "I gave him a quick dust-off. Partway through lunch, I took Reverend Clark to have a look at some Staffordshire pastoral pieces. That's when I discovered the window open, a trampled violet mess where my autumn crocus bed had been, and Sir Percival gone from his case."

"That's appalling," Miss Miller said. "I'm so sorry. You've been nothing but delightful to us."

"There's no need to apologize, Mary. It's nothing to do with you."

"It's kind of you to say that, but I wonder if you'd mind if I spoke to the staff. It's just possible one of them might have spotted something useful."

"Oh?" Leona gave her a doubtful look. "I
suppose it's worth a shot. Do you want to
talk to everyone?" She called loudly for the
butler, Bierce.

"Let's start with people who might
reasonably have been outside. They'd have
had the most opportunity to see someone
wandering around."

"As good a place as any."

The butler knocked, and entered the
room. He was a tall, slender fellow of middle years, somewhat balding,
with a face that reminded Miss Miller a little of a miserable spaniel.
"Yes, ma'am?"

"Have you been outside today, Bierce?"

"No, ma'am. The day so far has been perfectly invigorating indoors."

"Very good. Could you find the gardener and his fellow, and
David—the coachman, not my nephew—and fetch them in here?"

If Bierce found the instruction odd, he kept it well hidden. "Yes,
ma'am. I will return with them shortly." He turned on his heel and left
the room.

"Oh well," Leona said. "He thinks I'm quite dotty anyway,
I suppose."

"Keep your fingers crossed," Miss Miller told her. "You'd be
surprised at how much some people spot without really knowing."

Ten minutes later, Bierce knocked again, and led in the three men.
"The men you requested, ma'am."

"Thank you, Bierce. Mary, this is Mr. Darden, our gardener, his
assistant Barry Ray, and our coachman, David Wells. Gentlemen, this
is Miss Miller. She'd like to ask you a few questions."

The trio made for an interesting set of contrasts. Darden had to be in his sixties, with a shock of white fluffy hair and a short, patchy beard. He was dressed in rough, grass-stained blue overalls and big hobnail boots that would undoubtedly leave enough mess behind him to have the cleaning staff in fits of dismay. Bits of dark leaf clung to him everywhere except in his hair. He looked deeply uncomfortable.

Barry, his assistant, was probably in his twenties and gave the impression of being unused to public company. The man had short deep-brown hair and watery eyes, with a clean-shaved chin. He was dressed in overalls as well, green where Darden's were blue, and newer. His lower legs and boots were speckled with purple, and his sleeves splashed with fresh mud. He appeared quite bemused.

David, the coachman, was comfortably middle-aged, and his outfit was clean, neat, and free of wear and tear. He carried himself with care, not quite a military deportment, but nevertheless suggesting quiet attention and competence. His light brown hair was much like his beard, a little on the long side, but not shabbily so. He wore an attentive expression.

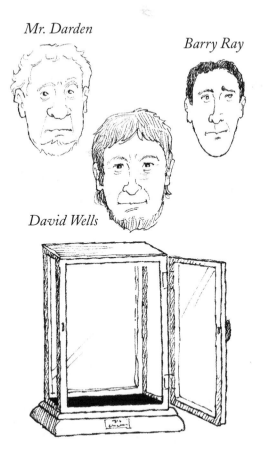

Mr. Darden

Barry Ray

David Wells

"Thank you for indulging me, gentlemen," Miss Miller said. "I wonder if any of you saw any guests outside but away from the main party this morning?"

There was a long moment of silence, then Barry spoke up. "I did think maybe I see'd a gentleman nip behind a bit of hedge this morning, ma'am. I didn't think nothing of it. Those birdy types can be a bit queer sometimes. Um. Begging your pardon, ma'am."

David frowned. "Was he wearing a dark suit and a tall hat, Mr. Ray?"

Barry nodded. "I think so."

"Around eleven?" David asked.

"Yes sir, that's about right."

Mr. Darden grimaced, and made a rumbling noise deep in his throat. "I didn't see nothing save the hedges I been pruning all morning. Gentlemen creeping around the gardens. Feh."

Barry flushed.

David shot the older man a glance. "Would you say that the man looked to be about five feet eight, Mr. Ray?"

Barry nodded, looking downcast.

"That's very helpful," Miss Miller told them. "Bierce, would you and the men excuse us for just one moment?"

The butler nodded, and led the trio back out of the room.

She turned to Leona with a smile. "That went better than I'd hoped. I suspect we'll have Sir Percival back in short order, and the Society thankfully off the hook as well."

Why does Miss Miller think that the thief is not a visitor?

HINT:

Movements.

THE FISHERMAN

№ 12

Eugene Mason had been found dead in the woodland behind his home, carrying a damp trio of heavy trout, a fishing rod, and a bait box, and wearing a bandolier of fishing flies. There were several rivers and fishable ponds within a couple of miles of the spot, and the quality of the man's gear suggested it had been one of his common pursuits. The path he was on was reasonably well used, enough to make backtracking his movements unlikely.

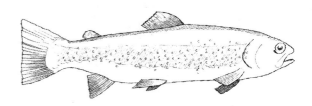

Inspector Parnacki looked the corpse over carefully. The cause of death seemed obvious—his chest, ruined by a close-range shotgun blast. Aside from that, and some signs of the morning's earlier rain

shower, there did not appear to be any other wounds. His hands were callused but undamaged, with no abrasions or bruises that might have suggested a fight. His face was calm and similarly unmarked, and his clothes appeared in good order, except for the damp and the gun damage.

Straightening up, the Inspector took a deep, slow breath. The scent of the forest around him was strong, wood and leaf and soil stirred by the early afternoon sun, with nothing but a faint smell of blood lingering beneath it all.

According to the notes prepared for him, Mason had been a quietly rugged man, the sort who minded his own business and preferred the great wilds of nature to the comforts of a pair of slippers and a pipe. He had no close family, and had earned his keep as an artisan, working mostly in wood and stone—tables, chairs, and other simple items of solid, dependable furniture. Although he'd been by no means wealthy, he'd had a small, enthusiastic following who appreciated his work, and his pieces had reliably sold almost as quickly as he produced them.

William Cox had been the man's only nearby resident for some years, and was the one who had found the body. After looking over the murder scene, the Inspector went to speak to Cox in his own home.

"It's a horrible waste," Cox said. "Gene was a very talented guy. Quiet, competent, you know the type."

Parnacki nodded. "How did you come to find the body?"

"I feel terrible about it, actually. Yesterday evening, just a little after sunset, I heard a faint shout, and then a shotgun went off. I figured it was someone after a bit of game, that's common enough round these parts, and went on about my business. During the night, though, I realized that there was something I hadn't entirely liked about the tone of the shout I'd heard. So this morning, when I went for my walk, I decided to just head up in that direction for a change. You can imagine the shock I had when I found poor Gene just lying there. I ran back to call you guys immediately."

"Were you friends?"

"Kind of, yeah. I mean, I knew him as well as anyone, but that wasn't all that well. He was never really easy in company. I got the impression his hearing was a bit lacking, and it made him awkward. He was perfectly nice, just happier on his own, you know? If he'd been a bit more at ease, he could have been a wealthy man—open a workshop, take on a couple of journeymen, turn his scrapings into a serious business."

"Scrapings?"

"That's what he called them. His furniture and other bits. Scrapings. He never really knew why other folk liked them, but then I suppose there was a lot he didn't understand about other folk. He had a great eye for wood." Cox gestured around the room, taking in an austerely handsome worked oak table, two comfy-looking log-carved chairs, a surprisingly intricate painting frame, and various other attractive items. "He'll be missed."

"I'm sure," the Inspector said. "William Cox, I'm arresting you for the murder of Eugene Mason."

Why does Inspector Parnacki suspect William Cox?

HINT:

Time.

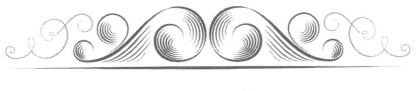

GAS

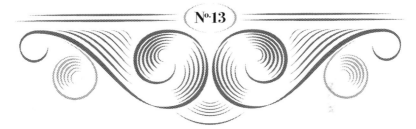

The Merrow Chemical Works was unknown to the public at large, but well respected among makers of medicines and pharmaceutical preparations. At least, that was what the company's general manager, Basil Elder, had told Emma Warren. "We are known for our purity, so all our supplies have to be of the finest grade. Unfortunately, this makes them a very tempting target for discerning thieves."

Emma had nodded. "Greater purity, greater value, I assume."

"Yes, and sometimes the relationship is logarithmic rather than linear—certain compounds are difficult to concentrate, and double the purity can mean ten times the price. Some of our stocks are fantastically expensive, Mrs. Warren."

Which was why, after two successful thefts of small, expensive chemicals, Mr. Elder had increased security and changed access permissions, slowing the thefts somewhat but not stopping them. His next line of attack had been to retain Emma's services. At the same time, he sent most of the security team off for "emergency training", to bait the thief into striking. As an ostensible safety inspector, Emma had been given a long white coat, goggles, a clipboard, a pencil, and sufficient authority to wander anywhere in the entire works.

She had been nosing around the works amiably for two and half days, making notes on absolutely everything that seemed even vaguely interesting. She was in a laboratory when the evacuation sirens went off.

It was an impressive demonstration, and regularly rehearsed. Everyone in the room around her turned in eerie synchrony to face the door, and walked directly toward it at a brisk, even pace. They slotted through the door without any jostles, and into the larger corridor, merging smoothly with the traffic outside. Numbers picked up as they made their way toward the main entrance, but everyone maintained the same measured stride out into the yard.

As soon as she was outdoors, Emma peeled off to the left, away from the main flow of evacuees, and watched. She split her attention as best she could between the growing pool of workers in the yard, and those striding out to join them. The evacuees obviously had a system for where to wait, clustering in neat knots by some system unknown to her. As the flow started trickling off, she started to note discrepancies—one fellow actually running, another sauntering, a third, already out, looking sweaty and anxious.

Mustering her clipboard, she thought up a cover, and went to talk to the people she'd noted, starting with the runner.

"Emma Warren, Safety Procedures," she told him. "How was your evacuation process this afternoon?"

He blinked at her. "Reg Smith, Logistics. Nice to meet you. It was a bit of a nightmare, actually. I was all the way off in the B-corridor bathroom. I know we're not supposed to run, but with the whole building to get through, and no idea what or where the leak is, or whether it's intensifying or dissipating..."

She nodded. "Is there anything we could do to make your experience better?"

He thought about it. "Some variation in the alarm tone, perhaps? Some way of indicating the affected locations? There are three routes through from the back, and after the deaths in last year's chlorine leak, having to choose one was quite nerve-wracking."

"I'll be sure to pass that suggestion on," she said, making a mental note to do just that. "Thank you."

She moved on to the saunterer, who identified himself as Jared Alexander, from the engineering and maintenance team. "The process seems fine to me, thank you."

"You weren't concerned?"

"Of course not," he said. "Nothing to be worried about. All perfectly regular."

She thanked him, and made her way over to the anxious man.

"Emma Warren, Safety Procedures," she said.

He looked at her blankly. "What?" When she repeated herself, he stared for a moment. "Richard Koehler," he finally managed.

"Are you alright, Mr. Koehler?" she asked.

"What? Alright?" He took a breath. "Yes, yes, I suppose I am. There's a live reaction over a Bunsen-Desaga on my desk, and it might start a fire at any moment, but..." He paused. "But yes. I'm out here in fresh air, away from anything explosive, and I'm not poisoned. I *hate* these damned gas alerts. Thank you. Mrs... Warren, was it?"

"That's right," she said, smiling encouragingly. "If anything further happens, you won't be penalized for following procedure." *I hope*, she added to herself.

"I suppose not," he said. "I should try to relax, but I won't feel comfortable until I've contained the sample."

"Hopefully we'll get the all-clear soon," she said, and left him to his fretting.

Twenty minutes later, once everyone was back at their stations, she made her way to the Manager's office.

Mr. Elder looked up as she entered. "There's been another theft," he told her flatly. "The alarm was almost certainly cover. Please tell me you have something."

She nodded. "It's not conclusive, but there's someone I'm very suspicious of."

Who does Emma suspect of being the thief, and why?

HINT:

Reaction.

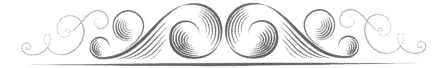

DEFENESTRATION

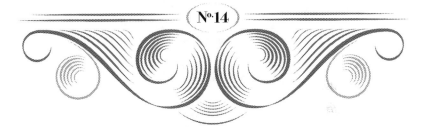

Nº·14

S imon Brake died in screaming terror, flung from a seventh-
floor window of a financial institution in the heart of the city's
business district. Despite the storm raging that evening, the
streets were busy, and a small horde of horrified onlookers had been
able to pinpoint the time of his death to precisely seventeen minutes
after seven. A number of witnesses also saw two men struggling at the
window in the moments before Brake fell.

Brake had been an inoffensive employee, according to the reports
handed to Inspector Parnacki. A pleasant enough man, somewhat
distractible and given to quiet flights of fancy and other daydreams.
He'd been with the firm for over a decade, and if his work had lacked
a certain inspired insight, it had also been reliable and solid. His
relationships with his colleagues had, for the most part, been amiable.
He'd seemed content enough in his role, on the lower edges of the
management structure. After some initial scepticism and wariness,
his peers had accepted that he was simply not particularly ambitious,

and left him to it. The general emotion felt by colleagues regarding his murder was one of bemusement.

His family were considerably more distraught at his loss, but they too found it difficult to imagine any motive for the killing. "Simon was an amiable man," his brother had said. "He disliked conflict, eschewed rudeness, and kept controversial opinions to himself. Plenty of people didn't really get him, but I can't imagine anyone hating him, let alone wanting to kill him. It simply can't have been personal."

According to the building's admission records, only one other person had been in the institution's offices at the time, a colleague of Brake's by the name of Berry, who now awaited the Inspector in the Interview Room.

Clutching his file, Parnacki made his way to the room where Mr. Berry was waiting. As soon as he entered, the chap levered himself painfully to his feet and limped forward a heavy step. "Inspector Parnacki in the flesh! It's a pleasure to meet you, sir. Glenn Berry, at your disposal."

Berry was a tall man, strongly built but going silver-haired, and he had a hearty, congenial voice. "Thank you," the Inspector said to him. "Please, be seated."

"Of course, of course." Berry lowered himself carefully back down into his seat, rubbing at his knee. He noticed the Inspector's glance, smiled ruefully, and gave his stout cane a pat. "Riding accident three years ago. Old news."

Parnacki nodded. "Yes, it's in the notes. I imagine you know why I've asked you here."

"Poor Simon, yes. Of course. Terrible shame. We worked in the same office. He was a delightful fellow, you know. Always whimsical.

Very interesting to talk to, so long as you didn't need any actual information." Berry chuckled to himself.

"And what was his job, precisely?"

"Our department deals with oversight, for the most part. Checking accounting figures, monitoring irregularities, looking for signs of trouble."

"Were you in the office that evening?"

Berry widened his eyes. "Me? My word, no! I'm quite religious about not working past six thirty. The King's Head on the corner of Bank Street has a beer ready for me at 6.35 without fail."

The Inspector shuffled his folder of notes. "According to building's ledgers, you signed out at 7.40 that evening."

"Ah. Yes, of course, the storm. Slipped my mind." His expression didn't waver, a perfect mask of innocent bonhomie. "I was there. I hid inside the file office for an hour to give the torrents a chance to blow over."

Parnacki looked at his notes. "My understanding is that the office manager locks the file office at five thirty."

The mask cracked and, just for an instant, panic shone out from behind the man's sociability. "He must have forgotten, the silly fellow. Lucky for me, eh!"

"So you didn't hear or see anything of the attack on Mr. Brake?"

"Not a thing, I'm afraid. I'd have given the scoundrels what for if I had, I'll tell you that."

The Inspector nodded. "Were you friendly with Mr. Brake?"

"Yes, of course. I mean, I wouldn't say we were ever bosom pals, you understand. I wouldn't have taken him fishing!" Berry guffawed at the idea. "No, no. But yes, he was perfectly pleasant. He did his job well enough, and what else could you ask for?"

"Did you ever go out drinking with him?"

Berry chuckled again. "With Breaker? Hardly."

"So you weren't with him and a young lady last week at the Helix Club?"

"Well... Yes, all right. I was. I wanted him to introduce me to Maggie, a new friend of his."

"Maggie?"

"Maggie Valle. She lives in a small house in Eastwood."

"I see," Parnacki said. "Have you seen Miss Valle since?"

Berry's expression frosted over. "I hardly think that's relevant."

"Please answer the question, sir."

The man frowned. "Surely you don't suspect me of being the murderer, Inspector? I didn't kill the man."

Parnacki sighed. "I'm well aware of that," he said. "But if you don't stop lying, it will go very poorly for you."

Why does Parnacki think Glenn Berry isn't the killer?

HINT:

History.

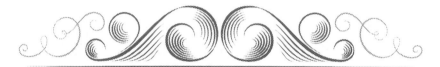

THE HALCYON
ROOMS

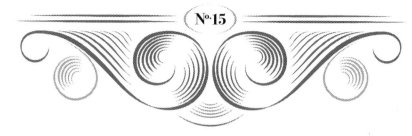

Nº·15

News of the murder of Sally Wilde had been splashed over the front page for two days. The glamorous actress had died in her dressing room while getting ready for a dress rehearsal, poisoned by persons unknown for reasons that so far remained mysterious. The press were, naturally, delighted, and there had been a steady flow of gossip and salacious insinuations ranging from the merely grubby to the outright peculiar.

Even so, Emma was a little surprised when the manager of the playhouse in which Miss Wilde had died retained her services. David Knowles was a patrician through and through, tall and clear-browed, with a strong chin, roman nose, and shock of thick, carefully tamed hair. He was obviously deeply flustered and confused, however, and the expression looked quite alien on his face.

Despite his distress, he managed to greet Emma courteously. "Mrs.

Warren, I am most grateful that you have been able to come to our assistance so promptly. Welcome to the Halcyon Rooms. Alas, that her name become such a misnomer. I am David Knowles, and I serve as her steward through the seas of fortune—and black misfortune."

Emma gave him a polite smile. "The pleasure is mine. I hope I can help."

"Oh, I do pray that it is so," he said. "The current situation is simply unbearable."

"Please forgive me if I'm being indelicate," she said carefully. "But I would usually expect the publicity around a case like this be beneficial for such an institution."

"Yes," Knowles said flatly. "But usually the police have not convinced themselves that the murderer is my sister."

"Ah."

"Ah indeed, Mrs. Warren. Lorna is a quiet and gentle woman, and benefits nothing from this extreme action. I cannot believe her guilty. I need you to find the truth."

"Why do they suspect her? Have they said?"

"Lorna is our resident genius in the art of make-up. She and Sally had been alone together for two hours when it happened, and cyanide, apparently, acts quickly."

"I think I'd better speak to her," Emma said.

"I think you had," Knowles agreed.

Lorna Avery was a striking woman a few years younger than her brother. She shared his height, but her features were more refined than his, giving her an aristocratic air of genteel determination. Her eyes were kindly, however, even through the obvious concern she felt.

"Sally Wilde was a leading actress through and through," she told Emma, "but it's an emotive calling. Her manner did not upset me, and her death does not help me in any way."

"I believe you," Emma said. "Perhaps you should talk me through the events of the morning as exactly as you can."

Lorna sighed. "Sally was playing a young, tragic mother, disfigured by old burns. She arrived at six a.m. for preparation. I washed and dried her hair, and brushed it back flat. While the creams were setting, I gave her face a thorough cleanse. Then we started with the wig, which of course didn't fit properly. It took about twenty minutes to seat it comfortably. Her nose and cheek prosthetic was a little late arriving from the specialist, which delayed us ten minutes or so, but it at least fit. I built up some additional old scars on her forehead with putty, then started with the cosmetics. There was a layer of foundation, then flesh-tone creams, some powders, and a blusher. I was putting on her eye-shadow when she started wheezing most alarmingly. That was a little after eight. She shot to her feet, wavered around, and dropped to the floor. She was dead before an ambulance could get to her. Cyanide, I was told."

Emma frowned. "Did she drink or eat anything?"

"Not a thing, I'm afraid. Not even tea."

"Could someone have tampered with the cosmetics?"

"It's extremely unlikely. I use the same items day in and day out. I didn't start any new vials or jars for her. The police confiscated my entire stock for testing, of course, even my costume putties and my shampoos. They won't find anything, though."

"Is there anything else they've taken?"

Lorna nodded. "My water pitcher and glass, which Sally didn't drink from, a bouquet of flowers from the table over there that she didn't so much as look at, a bowl of fruit from the hallway, and an unopened bottle of champagne that I think they just fancied the look of."

"Is there someone who might have wanted her dead?"

"My dear, this is showbiz. Actors are deeply passionate, deeply spiteful, and deeply deceitful. But there's no open rival I can point you to."

"So," Emma said thoughtfully. "She consumed nothing, had no contact with anything or anyone external, had no clear enemy, and was alone with you for two hours before dropping dead from a fast-acting poison. Is there anything that the police haven't taken into account?"

Lorna shook her head unhappily. "I'm afraid not. It looks very bad for me."

Emma blinked as a thought hit her. "Wait. There is something."

What is it that Emma has realized?

HINT:

Make-up.

THE
GEM SHOP

Nº 16

T he peeling sign above the gem shop read 'BALDWIN &
SONS', and if the date were to be believed, it had been in
business for more than thirty years. The window displays were
orderly, if empty, but the open door was hanging at an odd angle. A
bored-looking police officer stood in front of it. As Inspector Parnacki
approached, the man pulled himself properly erect and saluted sharply.

"Sir, good morning," he said.

Parnacki nodded politely. "Has anyone been in or out of the shop?"

"Not since I've been here, sir."

"Good work."

The robbery was much more obvious once Parnacki entered the shop.
Many of the cupboards showed signs of having been forced open and
empty trays were strewn all over the floors and glass counters. If there
was a single valuable jewel left in the place, it was well out of sight.

A tall, unhappy man stood in the middle of the chaos. He was well dressed, but in some considerable disarray, and there was a nasty-looking bruise at the side of his forehead. Parnacki went straight to him.

"Mr. Henry Baldwin?" the Inspector asked.

The man nodded.

"I am Inspector Parnacki."

Baldwin looked surprised. "Paddington Parnacki?"

"So the newspapers dub me," the Inspector sighed.

"Sorry, Inspector. Your fame precedes you."

"No matter. Would you please tell me what happened, in your own words?"

Baldwin nodded. "I was closing up last night. Sometimes one of my assistants stays behind to help, but they were both keen to get off swiftly. Their names are Alec Cardue and Scott Benedict. I have their addresses."

"The events of last night first, please," said Parnacki.

"Sorry. I'm still a little rattled. I'd finished locking all the precious pieces away—" he gestured at the broken cupboards, "—and turning the lights off, and I was just opening the door to start barring the windows. As I did so, a dark figure in a tall hat crashed through the door, throwing me back. I staggered, and then he hit me hard on the head with a cosh of some sort. I didn't get a good look at him. It was night already, you see. Anyhow, I fell over, and cracked the back of my head on the floor. Drove the wits from me. I was dimly aware of the noise of the cupboards being broken into. I didn't realize until later that he was also grabbing the trays and tipping the contents into his silk sack.

It all seemed disconnected, somehow. I must have passed out at some point. When I came round, it was already light. I remembered the assault, discovered that I'd been totally cleaned out, and called the police. That was about an hour and a half ago."

Parnacki nodded. "You mentioned your assistants?"

"It feels like an inside job, you know? I had bought a new batch of stock three days ago, and anyway, you'd need to know my routine to judge exactly when to break in like that. It seems impossible to imagine either of them doing this, but they're both around the right build. Alec has a new girlfriend too, and Scott likes his cards."

"Don't concern yourself, Mr. Baldwin. I already know the culprit."

"You do?"

Parnacki nodded gravely.

Who is the thief? How does Parnacki know?

HINT:

Testimony.

FRIDAY NIGHT SPECIAL

Nº 17

K al Knox died on Friday night. Several witnesses in the area heard the gunshot, placing the time of death at shortly after ten o'clock. Inspector Parnacki wasn't particularly surprised by the news. A low-rent career criminal, Knox had been violent, and although he had managed to avoid any murder convictions, he had never been likely to enjoy a long life. Appearances suggested that Knox had been going to a meeting of some sort. There was a note in his breast pocket, and although the bullet had ripped through it and blood had turned it into a soggy mess, the time 10.15 could still be made out.

The bullet that had been pulled out of him was a .38, and it matched the revolver the police had found in an industrial trash container a block away. It had been wiped down, but the lab was going over it to see if anything useful came up. In the meantime, three likely candidates had been brought in for questioning, and were waiting

for Parnacki in separate
interview rooms.

Lorenzo Holbrook was a local
restaurateur with unproven ties to the
mob. He was in his fifties and medium height
with a stocky build. Bushy silver hair did nothing to
disguise his calculating eyes.

Parnacki introduced himself and slapped a photo of the victim in
front of Holbrook. "Do you know this man?"

Holbrook nodded. "Yeah. Knox, ain't it? He comes in the Olive
Grove sometimes. Lousy tipper."

"Can you think of anyone who might wish Mr. Knox harm?"

"Nah. Can't say I know anyone who wishes him well either, mind."

"He was murdered last night."

Holbrook shrugged. "Is that so? Tragic. Tragic."

"What were you doing around 10 pm last night?"

"Washing dishes," said Holbrook. "What else? I got three staff
will vouch for it. I saw someone run down the alley behind my place,
though. Little ferrety guy in a hat. It was dark. That's the best I can do,
Inspector."

Toby Black was a cab driver who had done a stint in prison for
armed robbery years before. "I was waiting for a fare who never showed,"

he explained. "Dispatch will tell you that. I saw your guy, must've been. He hung around for a bit, then checked the time and walked into an alley. It was just across the road from me. A moment later, a tall man in a heavy coat walked in behind him. I remember, because the newcomer was as bald as an egg. There was a pop, and your victim just collapsed. Poor guy never even got the chance to turn round. Then the bald man sprinted off past him, down the alley. I was going to go and see if I could help, really I was, but I was scared in case the bald guy decided to come back to double-check. If there's one thing driving a cab has taught me, it's that you don't go looking for trouble. Not in this town."

The final interviewee, Jesse Hamby, worked in a local bar. Tall and muscular with short hair, he didn't bother hiding his resentment at being called in. When Parnacki showed him the photo, he shook his head silently.

"Are you sure?" asked Parnacki.

"Sure? Hell, no," Hamby sneered. "I see four hundred different guys in the bar every week."

"What were you doing around 10 pm last night?"

"Walking home."

"Did you see or hear anything unusual?"

"You mean apart from a chunky old guy who almost smacked into me, and what looked like a dead man huddled in an alley? Nope."

Parnacki sighed. "What can you tell me about the dead man?"

Hamby tapped the photo. "You got his picture already."

"Thank you, Mr. Hamby. I'll be back shortly." Inspector Parnacki rose and left the room.

Outside, he turned to the officer guarding the interview rooms. "Make sure no one leaves. I have an arrest warrant to finalize."

Who is the murderer, and how does Parnacki know?

HINT:

Wound.

THE FOREMAN PIECES

Nº·18

"They knew just what they were looking for, Mary." Stella's eyebrows were knotted in irritation.

Miss Miller clucked sympathetically. "Would you like some more tea, my dear? What a horrible business this must be for you."

Stella Simmons pushed her cup and saucer over. "It is horrible, yes. That's a good word. Losing the pieces is annoying, but that's not the thing. One feels so . . . invaded."

It had been two days since the break-in. Three expensive Foreman statuettes had been seized, but nothing else.

"That does fade, I promise you," Miss Miller said. "It takes some time, though. You might want to hire some extra help to keep watch on things for a few weeks. Although I'm sure they won't be back. They got what they wanted. Foreman is very desirable at the moment, so there's quite a bit of his work on the market."

"Don't I know it," Stella said. "The police were quite pessimistic. Said it would be a devil of a chore to positively identify my pieces if they've already been sold on. Which, they think, they will have been."

"Have you had much trouble with the press?"

"Oh, them." Stella sighed. "Blasted idiots couldn't get anything right. Spelled Simmons with a 'd', claimed I'd lost five pieces, and utterly fabricated a supposed quote about how 'utterly distraught' I was to have lost 'priceless family heirlooms packed with memories'. Complete nonsense. I'm obviously not happy, but I got the damned things last winter because they were attractive."

"Any idea how they knew where to look?"

"Oh, I don't think they did. They went through several rooms downstairs, poking around. They only wanted the Foremans."

"I suppose it's no secret you liked his work."

"Not since I agreed to that dratted interview a few months ago, no. What the contents of my home has to do with migrating plovers, I have no idea."

"I think they call it scene-setting," Miss Miller said. She paused. "Oh, Aubrey, no, not on the table. It's just tea, sweetie." She picked her cat up from where he was nosing at her cup, and set him back down on the floor.

Stella managed a weak grin for the cat.

"I'm not promising anything," Miss Miller said. "However, I do know a couple of local antique dealers who have a reputation for underhand dealing. I may have a little nose around."

"Goodness, you are brave! Thank you, my dear."

Miss Miller smiled thinly.

Later that afternoon, she found herself standing outside Coombs, a rather down-at-heel antique shop of her acquaintance. Pride of place in the window display was claimed by a handsome Foreman piece. It certainly could have been one of Stella's, but it could just as easily have come from elsewhere.

She had barely taken five steps into the shop when Eli Coombs materialized. The owner of the shop, he was an oily man in his early sixties, given to cheap beige suits.

"What a delight to discover such a charming lady in my humble boutique," Coombs declared, making a sweeping bow. "How may I be of assistance?"

"I'm interested in the Foreman," Miss Miller told him.

"Oh, of course. What a wonderful eye you have. It's a lovely piece of work."

"I trust that you can verify its provenance."

"Of course, Madam. Every piece I stock is fully documented."

Miss Miller nodded. "I hope so. Given the recent Simmons burglary, one can't help but wonder."

"My dear lady, are you seriously trying to suggest..." Coombs' smile had vanished, and his accent had thickened quite noticeably, too.

"Mr. Coombs, I am not your dear anything. Is that one of the stolen statuettes?"

"Preposterous!" Coombs spluttered. "I would never be party to such roguery. You could search everything I own from top to bottom and never find a hint of the other two. I can't remember ever being quite so insulted. Please leave at once."

"My apologies," Miss Miller said. "I meant no insult. I shall take my leave."

Exiting the shop, she went straight to the police station, and told the duty officer, "I can tell you who's fencing the goods stolen from the Simmons burglary."

How does she know that the statuette is definitely stolen?

HINT:

Reportage.

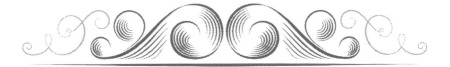

THE MISER

No. 19

Walking briskly through the park, Inspector Parnacki took a long draw on his pipe and tried to clear his mind.

Fact: Karson Meyers was dead and, apparently, almost completely unlamented. Fact: Meyers had been stabbed through the throat with a poker snatched from beside the fire in his sitting room. Fact: Time of death looked to be somewhere between 7 pm and 11 pm. Fact: The maid had caught sight of Meyers lying on the floor in a pool of blood shortly before breakfast and raised the alarm. Fact: She had told a number of curious inquirers that the murder weapon had been a poker before he'd had a chance to ask her to stop, unfortunately. Fact: Half a dozen people had motive to want the old miser dead, the opportunity to have done it, and a reasonable if flimsy alibi. Fact: Having interviewed all six, he didn't seem to be any closer to identifying a suspect.

Such a state of affairs irked the proud Parnacki. Puffing on his pipe, he thought back on the various interviews.

Michael Knight was a lumber distributor, and one of Meyers' most vocal creditors. The two had been doing business for several years, but Meyers now owed him a substantial sum of money. According to Knight, Meyers had steadfastly refused to settle the debt. "I'm not surprised someone did him in," Knight had said. "He was infuriating. It wasn't me, though. I was at home with my wife all evening. Besides, I don't hold out hope of getting any money out of his estate. Unfortunately, he owed me the money personally, rather than through his firm."

Susan Hugo was Meyers' long-estranged daughter, his only child. She was having a difficult time of it financially, and might possibly have hoped that she would be the main beneficiary of whatever her father had to leave. "I'd love to feel sad that he's dead," she had said. "One ought to feel sad when one's father dies. But the truth is that he was never pleasant to me or my mother. I haven't been alone in a room with him since Mother died, and that was fifteen years ago. But being murdered with a poker, that's horrible. I suppose I feel a bit sad about that. My husband, Paul, is sick at the moment. I was looking after him. I understand that you have to ask. He'll confirm my alibi."

Ian Goddard, one of Meyers' managers, was unusually forthright in his interview. "I'm absolutely delighted that the old son of a bitch is dead. He was a coward, a bully and a skinflint, and he made my life miserable. Maybe now we'll have a chance of getting the firm back onto a firm footing. I thought about killing him myself, you know. Repeatedly. But he wasn't worth it. I was playing bridge last night, with three friends. I can even give you a run-down of how the hands played out, if you want."

Evan Patterson was the other manager. He seemed more reflective than bitter about the victim. "It's difficult to think of him as dead, let alone stabbed. He was such a dominating presence. He only had to walk into a room, and it seemed as though all the air vanished. We shouldn't speak ill of the dead, but God help me, I won't miss him. The company won't miss him, either. I suppose we'll have to put out some regretful-sounding statement and have an official day of mourning or something. I had dinner with my brother last night."

Emma Moss was Meyers' housekeeper. Her interview was short and to the point. "Heard he was dead." Pressed on her whereabouts for the evening in question, she grudgingly added "Home, of course, with my family."

Jerrold Stanton was Meyers' butler. "I never had an employer like Mr. Meyers. Oh, my. What a broken man. I tried to leave, six years ago, as soon as I realized exactly what sort he was. He made it clear that if I did, he'd accuse me of theft and bribe the judge to send me to prison. I never dared even hint of leaving again. It's been hard, but I kept my head down, and did as I was told. It's time for a new chapter in my life. I was at the bar last night, having a beer or two."

Parnacki suddenly stopped dead. "Stupid of me," he said. "Stupid!" He immediately turned on his heel, and hurried back toward the station.

Who is the killer, and how does Parnacki know?

HINT:

Poker.

VICTOR'S
FUNERAL

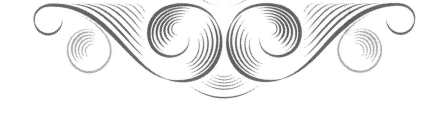

Nº·20

Victor Ivanova had a rather successful funeral, all things considered. The service was appropriately moving, the burial went smoothly, and they even managed to find some people to say kind things about him. His evil temper and ready fists were glossed over as a "passionate nature". Apparently, getting shot earned one a certain measure of posthumous tolerance.

At the wake afterwards, Miss Miller availed herself of some tea and a small crustless sandwich and set out to circulate. Although the police had yet to rule on whether Victor had committed suicide or been murdered, his supposed mourners seemed to have very little collective doubt.

"Of course he was murdered!" At just 20, Kailee Williams was still rather excitable, and seemed to be enjoying herself thoroughly. Her beau, Eugene, was Victor's son. "It's wrong to speak ill of the dead, but poor dear Eugene suffered terribly for his father's moods. But so many

others did, too. Men like Victor don't commit suicide. They don't have the self-awareness. They just hang around forever, getting older and meaner and older and meaner. I bet it was the gardener. Victor actually whipped him, once. Can you imagine? Whipping a gardener? It chills the blood, I tell you."

Chance Hoffs was a long-standing friend of the family. "Victor always was a difficult man," he said. "He got worse as the years ticked by. I don't think I'll ever really know what was sticking in his craw, but the frustration and anger seemed to grow. He made it to his forties, which honestly is about as far as most people ever expected. I don't suppose we'll ever really know the truth of it. The nearest thing to a witness was his great-aunt in the next room, but she's as deaf as a stump, and didn't hear a thing."

Eventually, Miss Miller tracked down Victor's great-aunt, Agatha, to a sunny corner of the room. She was a spry-looking octogenarian with bright, lively eyes and a large ear trumpet.

"Hello. I'm Mary Miller," said Miss Miller, joining Agatha at her table.

The old lady held up a forbidding finger, then laboriously swung the ear trumpet into place, jamming one end into her ear, and pointing the other directly at Miss Miller's mouth. "What was that, my dear?" Her voice was surprisingly steady.

"I said hello, and that my name is Mary Miller."

"Agatha Ivanova. Delighted to meet you. Did you know my great-nephew?"

"Socially," said Miss Miller.

"Ah, by far the best way. Poor man. There were devils inside him, you know." She paused. "Metaphorical devils, that is, not literal ones. I haven't lost my mind just yet. Victor could be quite charming when everything was going his way. He never could bear to be thwarted. But then his father, my nephew, was quite the tyrant in his time. It's so silly, this violence and scorn that men heap on their sons."

"Eugene seems quite nice," Miss Miller said.

"Yes, indeed. He was shielded by his mother—literally, often. Victor's violence was relatively easy to deflect, if one were prepared to pay the cost. There is marble in that woman's spine, I tell you."

Recalling Briony Ivanova's firm, composed appearance at the funeral, Miss Miller could only agree. The widow was toward the middle of the room at the moment, talking with several guests. A bellow of anger erupted from the far side of the room. Agatha and Miss Miller looked round together. A weathered-looking man was being calmed by several other people.

"Victor's gardener," Agatha said. "He has a lot to be angry about."

"Do you think he might be the killer?"

Agatha's eyebrows raised at that, and she chuckled. "Well, I suppose he might be. No use asking me, my dear."

"You were in the next room," said Miss Miller.

"Quite so, but I'm afraid I was reading. If anyone walked past my door, I didn't see them."

"So you didn't hear any arguments?"

"I didn't even hear the gunshot," Agatha said. "I wouldn't hear the last trump itself unless I was pointing this beast straight at it." She patted her ear trumpet with her free hand.

"No, of course," Miss Miller said. "But you must have some suspicions."

Agatha nodded. "Honestly, I suspect he died by his own hand. I like to imagine that he had a moment of lucidity, and realized that the only way to stop himself from destroying his son was to end his own life. One concluding moment of actually being a father." She sighed. "I'm glad that Eugene has that nice Miss Williams to help him through this. She reminds me a little of his mother—kind and bright, with a core of steel. I'm quite sure you know the type, my dear." She shot Miss Miller a very knowing look.

Miss Miller smiled politely. Oh dear, she thought. Who are you covering up for, Agatha?

How does Miss Miller know that the old lady is lying?

HINT:

Gardener.

THE TIP

N⁰·21

M ary Miller poured two cups of tea, and passed one across
the table.

Jasmine Hillins took it gratefully and had a distracted
sip. "It's not that anyone has complained, you understand."

"Of course," said Miss Miller.

"Word does get around though, doesn't it? To have a thief on the
staff..."

"Why don't you tell me about it from the beginning, my dear?"

Jasmine sighed. "Oh, Mary. I couldn't burden you like that."

"Nonsense. It's the least I can do."

"Well, if you insist...

Last Saturday, Hayden threw a little party for some of his pals from
the club. There were maybe twenty of us in all, including the wives.
As we were saying goodbye to everyone, Mrs. Snell sent a message
that she needed to see me immediately. I thought maybe there were
problems with the following day's arrangements, but no. She'd caught

a glimpse of one of the kitchen girls, Hailey Johnson, lurking in the
pantry and tucking a large banknote into her purse. She called the girl
over, and demanded to see her purse. Hailey turned it over sullenly,
and there it was. Over a month's worth of her pay!"

"Shocking," Miss Miller said, suppressing the urge to ask how little
Hayden paid the girl.

"Quite. I could hardly ask
Hayden to call everyone and
inquire as to whether they had
been robbed of a substantial
amount of money under
our roof. Hailey insists
that the note was

tucked between pages 69 and 70 of a book which someone had placed on her tray. She says she didn't notice who it was, because she was busy collecting glasses. The wretched girl insists that it's a gift, a consideration from one of the gentlemen who didn't want to be spotted giving her a little something while his wife was around."

"Does she now?"

"I know! Of course, I'd hardly put it past some of Hayden's friends. Well, to be honest, I wouldn't entirely put it past any of them. Boys will be boys. But it's a very generous gift for just handing out the champagne, if you know what I mean. There must be more to it than that."

"Yes. Did you have a look at the book in question?"

"Well, yes. It's a dreadful volume by some Irish fellow, full of blood and bodices and suspicious Eastern European noblemen. One of Hayden's. But it definitely is his copy, and it was clearly just taken from a bookshelf. There's no useful information to be gleaned there, I tell you."

"I see," said Miss Miller.

"Hayden's spoken to everyone without asking them directly, asked if they had a pleasant evening, that sort of thing, but no one seemed in the least bit put out. They all claim to have had an absolutely divine time, of course. None of them mentioned Hailey, either."

"Unfortunately, I think you may have to take this one at face value, Jasmine. Keep a careful eye on the girl, but unless someone speaks up, I don't see what else can be done."

Once Jasmine had gone, Miss Miller penned a short, anonymous note to Hailey Johnson:

I dare you deserved one little windfall, but I am watching. Steal anything again from the Hillins or their guests, and I'll drag you to the police station myself.

– Vigilant.

She sealed it, arranged to have it delivered discreetly, and went on about her business.

How does Miss Miller know that the money is stolen?

HINT:

Book.

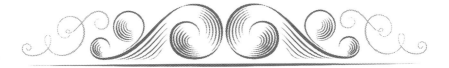

THE NARCISSIST

Nº·22

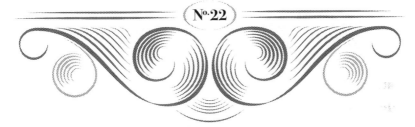

I nspector Parnacki tapped the stem of his pipe thoughtfully
against his palm. Aiden Pearce had been unusually unpopular,
even among murder victims. A crashingly narcissistic bore with
poorly managed criminal tendencies, he had generally operated on the
right side of the law—enough so that the police had never been able
to charge him with anything, anyway. When
informed of his death, his
young wife had burst
into tears of relieved
joy, much to the officer's
discomfort. Parnacki
decided to interview her first.

Annabeth Pearce had
regained her composure when
Parnacki met her. Slender and twenty-
two, Annabeth had slightly bulging eyes

which gave her the appearance of a perpetually startled doe.

"I feel I must apologize for what I did this morning," she told him. "I know it is unseemly to speak ill of the dead, but my husband was exhausting to be married to, and often prone to terrifying moments of rage. He would never have let me go. When I heard the news, it felt as if my soul had been set free."

Parnacki nodded politely. "Of course. Can you think of anyone who would have wanted to kill him?"

Annabeth laughed bitterly. "Anyone who'd spent more than five minutes in his company?"

"Quite. Anyone specific?"

"No more so than usual," Annabeth said. "Not that I know of."

"I'm sure you understand that I have to ask where you were between 7.30 and 8.30 this morning."

She nodded. "I was at the market, buying food and other necessaries. Everything had to be purchased fresh every morning, in case he came home for lunch, and then again in the afternoon, for dinnertime. The wastage was staggering. There are several stallholders I shop from every day who can confirm I was there."

Michael Solis, Aiden's assistant, was in his early thirties. He was a wary, tired-looking man, prematurely balding, with a sallow cast to his skin.

"I found the body, yes," Solis told Parnacki. "Pearce always got in before 7.30. The rest of us were under strict instructions not to arrive before 8.30. He liked an hour in the morning to work privately. I immediately knew he was dead. He was slumped face down over his desk, blood pooling out over everything."

Parnacki nodded. "Can you think of anyone who might have wanted to murder Mr. Pearce?"

"He was a self-obsessed cheat and bully," Solis said. "Never popular traits, and particularly not in a freewheeling trader. Personally I loathed him, but his death is inconvenient—I'll have to find another job. I was at home with my fiancée until 8.10, as always, and then I came straight here."

Anthony Stewart was Pearce's bookkeeper. Tall and thin, and a few years older than Solis, he had something of a librarian about him. When he spoke, it was with a precise, almost clipped accent.

"You must understand that I knew little of Mr. Pearce's actual business," Stewart said. "He generated a layer of obfuscation in order to avoid his subordinates gaining enough information to facilitate a betrayal. It's a shame, actually. I would have liked to have had a look at the shipping manifest he was working on."

"So you don't know of any specific enemy Mr. Pearce may have had?"

"I'm afraid not, no. He left lots of unhappy people in his wake. As for my movements, I was at home until 8.20 before arriving here at 8.45, as my wife will attest."

The final employee, Noah Parham, worked as a general office junior. Young and heavily muscled, Parham compensated for his lack of education with a hearty cheerfulness. He seemed utterly unbothered by the morning's events.

"Someone finally got the old dog," he said. "It was going to happen sooner or later. He wasn't very nice."

"Any idea who?" asked Parnacki.

"Lord, no. Could be anyone, really. No one had made any open threats recently that I'd heard of."

"And where were you from 7.30 this morning?"

"At the docks," Parham said. "Delivering a package. There's plenty there as will vouch for that."

Once Parham had left, Inspector Parnacki leant back in his chair. "Nice and straightforward," he said to himself.

Who does Parnacki suspect?

HINT:

Paperwork.

PRICE'S MISTAKE

№·23

There was a good reason, Inspector Parnacki thought, why most wills remained confidential. Benjamin Price had called his family together to inform them of changes he was considering to his will. Specifically, he informed each of them of how much they were due to receive under the current will, and then gave them until the following morning to justify that amount. If he didn't like their answer, he would instead leave their portion to a local charity which looked after homeless cats.

He was dead within ninety minutes, from a potent cocktail of poisons.

The bereaved were still in varying degrees of shock the following morning. Parnacki's first interviewee was Price's business partner, Shane Massey. A few years younger than Price, he had come along to the family meeting at Price's express request.

"I tried to talk Ben out of it," Massey told Parnacki sadly. "But he was determined to put them on the spot. I can't help thinking that if I'd done more... But Ben wanted to see their faces, you see. They didn't know that there was no way to pass the test. He'd already decided to give it all to the cats no matter what. He just wanted to watch them squirm and try to justify themselves, and then rip up the old will in their faces. An unworthy urge perhaps, but he's paid a very high price for it now. He was a good friend to me, and I'll miss him. I stayed at the house until the end of the meeting, but I left immediately afterwards, and went straight to my club. I was there until midnight. Just all a bit too much for me."

Sharon Price was Ben's third wife. Some thirty years his junior, she had taken the events of the previous evening particularly hard. "I just don't understand," she said. "I loved Ben. Why would he do something like this to me? Was it all some sort of peculiar joke? What will happen to me now?"

Inspector Parnacki gradually managed to help her understand that he himself had no answers to any such questions, and got her back to the details of the evening.

"I had no idea what the meeting was about," she said. "Then he dropped his bombshell, and left us to it. I don't think I moved from my seat for so much as a moment until Casey came shouting that Ben was dead. That was a little after nine. Alison, the maid, was there in case we needed anything, and she stayed with me. The others were in and out, apart from Mr. Massey, who was gone almost before Ben finished.

Casey kept me company for a while. He's very kind."

Casey Price was Ben's son by his first wife. Just a few years younger than Sharon, he lived in lavish apartments in the city. "Do? I suppose you could say that I'm an art appreciator, Inspector. I have a passion for beauty. Yes, I was taken aback by Father's declaration. He was an odd bird, though, always given to whimsy and calculated cruelty. A bit like those damned cats, I suppose. I significantly doubt that any answer I could produce would have been sufficient for the old coot—except that one, perhaps. Hm? Maybe a little worried, I suppose, yes. I'll probably have to talk to a pal and get set up in business of some sort. A bother. After Father's speech, Bianca and I went into the billiards room. We had a bit of a catch-up. The butler was there, I think. Anyway, she wanted to get a snack from the kitchen, so I came back to the library to see how poor Sharon was doing. She's rather lovely, don't you think? Like a porcelain angel. I sat with her for a while, but she was quite out of it. When I went looking for Father, I found him quite dead."

Bianca Connors was Casey's full sister. Two years younger than her brother, she was married to the son of a local papermill baron. "He was a nasty old fool," she said. "I never liked him, and I most certainly won't miss him. I'm glad he's dead, in fact. The only time he paid attention to me was when he had just inflicted some emotional hurt or other. It's a shame, though—I was looking forward to telling him that I neither needed nor wanted his money, his time, nor anything else to do with him. Once he'd finished his juvenile stunt and doddered off, I had a bit of a chat with Case, in the billiards room. Then I popped down to the kitchen and shared a couple of glasses of sherry with Mrs. Reynolds, the cook. She's always been the sanest person in this dashed madhouse."

Afterwards, Inspector Parnacki went to stroll around the ornamental rose garden, so that he could smoke a pipe and ponder the specifics of the case. He had been there about ten minutes when an officer bustled up with a report. Analysis suggested that Price had ingested the poison some three hours before his death.

Parnacki immediately brightened. "That clears it all up nicely," he said.

Who does Parnacki suspect of being the murderer?

HINT:

Timing.

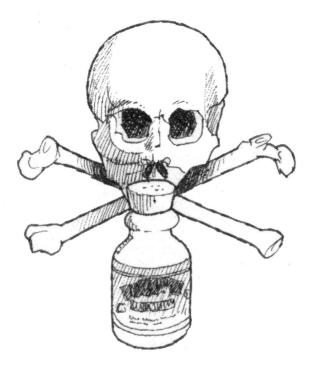

SOUTHWELL STOWE

№·24

As Christmas approached, Miss Miller found herself once again in charge of arranging the Ornithological Society's festive outing. In the end, she settled on Southwell Stowe, a venue which offered a range of peaceful, bird-friendly habitats on its lands as well as a rather good guest house. She arranged a meal and overnight stay with the couple who ran the guest house, and on the day of their outing the members of the society assembled at the venue shortly after dawn at 8 am before spreading out to enjoy their birdwatching.

Although the weather remained persistently cloudy, it never broke into rain or sleet. Miss Miller enjoyed a thoroughly pleasant and successful day, capped off by a spectacularly bright cardinal and a clear sighting of a hoary redpoll, quite a long way out of its usual winter territories. She stayed out until past 4 pm, and by the time she made it back, the guest house was a beacon of light in the glimmering darkness. She celebrated with a hot bath, followed by a fresh pot of tea.

Shortly before it was time to head down for dinner, there was a frantic knocking at her door.

"Come in," she called.

The door flew open. "Oh, thank goodness you're here, Mary." Isabella Walker was one of the younger members of the group, and prone to excitability. "It's terrible!"

"What's that, my dear?"

"It's Mr. Fonseca. He's been robbed!"

Miss Miller sighed with relief. "That certainly is bad," she said. "What happened?"

"I don't know," Isabella admitted. "Sara asked me to get you. They're in his room."

As it turned out, half the society were in Andrew Fonseca's bedroom. Eventually, Miss Miller managed to get them quietened down, and asked him to tell her what had happened.

"I was indulging in a little snooze," Andrew told her. "I didn't get back until 4.30. That's a long day for me. I didn't think to latch the door, of course. When I woke up, I discovered my watch and wallet had vanished. They were in my coat when I went to sleep, I'm sure of it. Some dastardly crook must have taken them."

Sara Amos leant in near Miss Miller's ear. "I'm next door. He was snoring like a grampus. Obvious target."

Miss Miller nodded. "Did anybody see anything suspicious? Someone prowling around, maybe?"

Blank stares all round.

"Excuse me," said an unfamiliar male voice behind her. "Mary Miller?"

She turned around to see David, the manager. "That's me," she told him.

"Did I hear correctly that there's been a theft?"

"Unfortunately, yes," she said.

"My dashed wallet!" called Andrew Fonseca.

"I'm so sorry," David said. "What a terrible impression you must have of us. I will contact the police immediately, and while we're waiting for them to arrive I'll question the staff to see if any of them knows something that might help. I'll also order complimentary cocktails to be served to you in the downstairs lounge. I do hope this won't spoil your stay too much. If there's any other way I might be of assistance, please just let me know."

Miss Miller thanked him, and he bustled off.

Ten minutes later, with the group enjoying their drinks, even Isabella Walker had calmed down somewhat. Miss Miller was reflecting on the day when David Southwell appeared at her shoulder again. "One of the maids saw something," he told her.

"Oh?" Miss Miller asked.

"Yes. She was in the dining room with several other girls, preparing it for dinner, when she saw a tall man with a dark complexion walk past, toward the road. She says she didn't think anything of it at the time, given the size of your group."

"That's interesting. Did she get a good look?"

"He had dark hair, and was wearing a red checked shirt, a heavy coat, and casual blue trousers. She didn't get a decent look at his face, though, as he was twenty or thirty feet away."

"I see. Are the police coming?"

"They'll have someone up here when they can, yes."

"Excellent. Please have them search her personal effects for the wallet and watch, would you?"

Why does Miss Miller want the witness's effects searched?

HINT:

Time.

MAYNARD'S

№25

T racey Kenyon had been painting woodlands and other natural scenes around the district for the best part of twenty years. The first time that Miss Miller had bumped into her, deep in a grove, it had been a bit of surprise to find an artist and easel in such an out-of-the-way location. Since then, Tracey had become a general friend of the Ornithological Society, and even came to events occasionally. Her art was popular with the society, and she was gaining recognition. She'd had a number of exhibitions in smaller galleries, but this was her first major showing, and Maynard's had put on quite the event to celebrate.

There was a luminous quality to Tracey's newer work, a sense of light and breath that gave the perfectly prosaic subject matter a sense of the numinous. Miss Miller was a frequent visitor to the small, wooded pond depicted in the piece in front of her. It was a pleasant spot, and in the spring quite lovely, but on the canvas in front of her it seemed almost a portal, a gateway to mysteries and wonders.

As she was pondering the precise alchemy of the transformation, Tracey appeared at her side, looking a little flustered. "Ah, Mary, there you are," the woman said. "I wonder if I might burden you with a little problem."

"Of course, my dear," Miss Miller assured her.

"If this seems odd to you, please just say, but you do have a certain reputation, so..."

Miss Miller smiled. "I do? How invigorating."

"My purse has been stolen from the small room that Maynard's set aside for my use. There were several personal things in there, but also a rather expensive pair of earrings and a matching necklace. There was a rough-looking florist's lad who arrived while I was in there, and I wonder... The manager has promised to call the police, but is disinclined to do so until the showing is over. I wonder, might you be able to lend me your famous eye for detail? I very much fear that the longer this waits, the less chance I have of getting anything back."

"You're quite right about that. Leave it with me, and try to enjoy the rest of this evening regardless. You've attracted quite the scene tonight, and you richly deserve the interest you're getting." She patted the woman on the hand reassuringly, and went to have a look around.

The nearest member of staff was a young woman holding a tray of wine glasses. Miss Miller went over to her. "Excuse me. Is there someone dealing with deliveries this evening? I just need to ask him something."

"Yes, madam. James Davies. He's taking care of the back end this evening. You can find him through there." She indicated a door.

"Not yourself, Miss...?"

"Terry. Sue Terry. No. Jordan and I are restricted to the main gallery this evening. I do normally handle artists' needs for showings, but Mr.

Maynard wanted extra feet on deck, so James stayed late. I'd have liked a chance to arrange those lovely flowers, but it wasn't to be. Would you like a glass of wine?"

"I'm fine, thank you," Miss Miller said. She bid the woman a good evening, and went in search of Mr. Davies.

Through the indicated door, there was a small room that appeared to be for staff breaks. It was empty, but a second door opened on to a stretch of comparatively plain corridor with several doors set along the further wall, and a double door at one end. There was a clatter, and a slightly dishevelled head popped out of one doorway. A moment later, the rest of the young man it was attached to followed it into the corridor.

He blinked a couple of times. "Um. Are you lost, ma'am?" he asked.

Miss Miller made a show of peering at him. "Are you James Davies?"

"Yes?"

She smiled. "Then I'm not lost. I'd like to ask you a couple of questions."

"All right," he said, evidently a little confused.

"You had a delivery of flowers for Miss Kenyon earlier? Tonight's artist?"

"That's right. About half an hour ago."

"Can you describe that delivery?"

Davies stared at her, clearly incredulous, then shrugged, mostly to himself. "Yes, ma'am. I was pouring Miss Kenyon some water, and I heard Davey's knock on the rear door. Davey is the florist's lad. No one else was around, so I opened the doors myself, ushered him through, and followed him to the artists' prep room. I knocked, opened the door when Miss Kenyon said, apologized to her, and had Davey vase up the arrangement quickly. Then I followed him out and back to the door, bid him a good night, gave him a coin for his troubles, and closed up again."

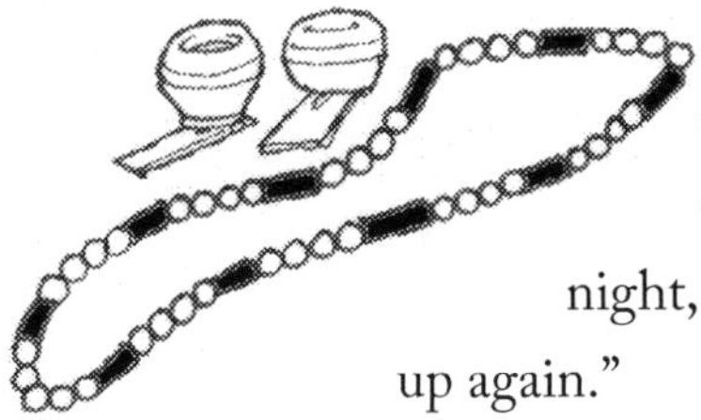

"Did he have any chance to pilfer anything?"

He blinked again. "Davey? Of course not. He's through here three days out of five, and has been for more than two years. But I was watching him, anyway. No way he swiped anything."

"I see. Has anyone else been back here since then?"

"Miss Kenyon left a few minutes after, and came back five minutes ago for a moment or two. That's it. Apart from your good self, I've seen no one else."

"You're certain?"

"Well, fairly, yes. I'm arranging pallets in the stock room, but I heard you walk in to the corridor readily enough."

Miss Miller smiled. "Thank you, James. You've been a great help."

"I have?"

"You have. You've solved a problem very neatly for me."

Why does Miss Miller say that James has solved her problem?

HINT:

Evening.

SCHAEFFER AND SONS

S chaeffer and Sons was one of the city's higher-end suppliers of clocks and watches. The shop's prestigious location close to the central entertainment district ensured a constant stream of traffic, and a solid reputation for quality provided a steady business. At 10.42 the previous evening, a patrolling policeman had spotted a large, short-haired man rushing out from the darkened premises with a hefty bag. He raised an immediate alarm, and although he was unable to apprehend the culprit, several men were stopped leaving the area a short while later, none with a bag. Those suspects now awaited interview. A note appended to the report indicated that later investigation determined a safe had been cracked open in the shop, and a considerable amount of money had been stolen, along with several small but valuable clockworks.

Inspector Parnacki was already in place in the interview room. He

set the report aside, and told
Sergeant Sullivan to send the
first of the suspects in.

The first man, Sep Knotte,
was in his thirties. He matched
the broad description of the
culprit—muscular, just short
of six feet in height, close-
cropped hair—but so did all the
potential suspects that had been
apprehended. He had several
crudely done tattoos visible
on his hands and neck, and he
appeared aggressively unhappy
at his night in holding.

"I'm on the docks, ain't I?"
he demanded of the Inspector.
"I don't have no truck with any
of that light-fingered stupidity.
Mug's game, that is. I work long
hours, and I work hard, and I earn every scrap that comes my way, and
my family don't go hungry or cold or unshod. That's the way it was for
my Da, and for me, and when I'm too broken to keep at it, that's the
way it'll be for my sons. So you be careful what you accuse me of, Mr.
Police Inspector. I won't have it, you hear?"

"You were a long way from the docks, Mr. Knotte," Parnacki
pointed out.

"And a long way from my home an' all. What of it? After a week on
late, I go for a few beers to take the edge back off. I was in the Green

Dragon on Highthorne Street and there's lots as saw me. Ginny, the barmaid, she knows me well enough. I wasn't even drunk enough to stagger, so you can't tell me you picked me up for that. I don't expect much, but I do expect to be free to mind my own ruddy business."

The second man was named Nick Spagnuolo, and he was more patient with the situation than Knotte had been. "I was on my way back from the playhouse," he told Parnacki. "A group of us had been to see a performance of *Much Ado About Nothing*. Lovely play, that is. I've got the receipt here, actually, if you'd like a look." He passed over a group-entry ticket stub priced sixty pence. "Who was I with? Friends, mostly ones I've known from childhood, one of them from Mason's. I'm a porter there, spend my day moving crates around mostly, keeping the crafters in supplies. I've had better jobs, but I've had worse, too. It doesn't stink, and that's nice. Yes, we do go to plays quite often actually. Once a month, when we can. Their names? Pete Smith, Danny Cook, Bill Dyer, Tom Chubb, James Corley, and Harry Hutton. Tom's the one from Mason's."

The third man, Albert Indon, looked utterly shattered. His skin was an unhealthy pallid tone, and he had big, dark patches under his eyes that made him look far older than his stated age of 43. He swayed slightly in his seat, apparently unaware that he was doing so, and when he spoke, his voice was slow and hollow. "I was walking, Inspector. Yes, alone, always alone. It is what I do. Sometimes it feels like I do not do anything else. I must have walked every street in this city over the last twenty years, many of them dozens of times. They blur together, you know. The houses and shops form walls of stone and brick, occasionally broken by the hungry eyes of windows. It is horrible. But it is better than lying in my room, watching the ceiling pulse. Sometimes, the real people are a distraction. Sometimes. Occasionally, if I walk far enough,

I am able to sleep a little. Do? I don't really understand. I walk. What else is there?"

Once the fellow had shambled away, Parnacki called his sergeant in. "We can send a pair of them home right away," he told the man. "Our lad's hoisted himself on his own petard."

Which of the men does Parnacki suspect of being the thief?

HINT:

Explanations.

THE PHILLIPS SUITES

Fergus Iver was the on-site manager for The Phillips Suites, a long, low complex of sheltered homes for elderly persons. Mr. Iver and his team provided assistance to the residents as required, but otherwise left them to their business. The rent was on the higher side, but places were quite sought after amongst certain independently minded members of the aging middle class.

Iver himself was in his fifties, a slight man who looked to have a somewhat nervous disposition. Currently, he was significantly unhappy. "It's not just horrible, Mrs. Warren. It is a betrayal of the trust our residents place in us. It is imperative that we bring this criminal to justice as swiftly as possible."

"Of course, Mr. Iver," Emma assured him. "You have a log of visitors from the afternoon in question?"

"Here," he said, and passed over a short list. "A visiting care

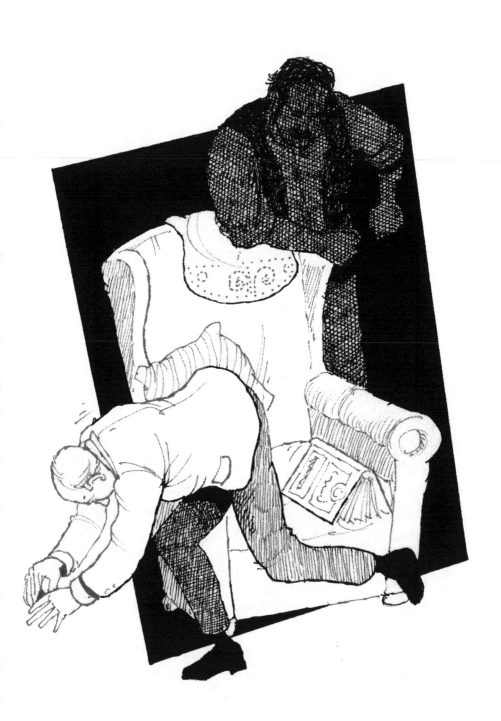

assistant, a delivery man, and a relative of the victim's nearby resident. I've included addresses for where you should be able to find them. I truly hate to imagine any of them responsible, however."

"Could someone have got in without being noted?"

"Over a wall, maybe." Iver sighed. "It's not impossible."

"It's always worth speaking to the people you know were in the area. I'll start by interviewing them. You yourself saw or heard nothing?"

"I'm afraid not. My office doesn't look out over Mr. Wallis's bungalow."

"Does Mr. Wallis remember the attack?"

Iver's expression darkened. "Not clearly. He's recovering, but he's still quite uncertain about much of it. He was quite thoroughly beaten, and an arm was broken. In addition to his cash savings, the assailant also took some silver forks, his ivory-handled cane, his wooden dentures, a selection of old army medals, and a bronze statuette of an ape of some sort. It's a significant loss for the poor fellow. He's very scared, still."

"I understand," Emma said. "I won't intrude on him unless there is no other option."

"I appreciate that," Iver said. "Good luck."

Ted Lawrence did deliveries for Thoroughgood's, a local grocery and the nearest address on the list. He proved to be an ungainly man of around her age, tall and thin-haired with a prominent Adam's apple, and a nasty cut on his left hand. He appeared to find her questions annoying, but kept his answers pleasant enough. "Yes, I was up the Phillips houses on Tuesday, twice in fact, like I usually am. Yes, a little before three. Mr. Wallis? Zeke. Yes, I saw him. Dropped off some fruit for him. He was fine. Yes, I saw some other bloke around the place.

Don't know who he
was, though. I dunno,
under 40? I didn't hardly
look at him. This cut?
Caught it on a loose nail on a packing box yesterday. Do you want me
to show you the box? Thought not. I'll get back to work, then. Good
day."

Edward Kendrick was the grandson of Ezekiel Wallace's nearby
resident, Charity Kendrick. Emma found him at a construction site,
and at his foreman's nod, he set down the very large stack of planks
he was carrying, and ambled over. He was a big man of 20 or so, his
face already seamed, and his hands and forearms covered with bruises,
scratches, and even a purpling bite. "Yeah, I was at my gran's a couple
of days ago. I go see her sometimes, days off. In the afternoon, yeah.
Left around three, I 'spose. No, I didn't hear anything from the old
coot next door. No, I didn't see no one lurking around neither. All as
quiet as a graveyard. My hands? Normal for my line of work, that is.
Yeah, that includes having to smack some mouthy sod in the teeth.
Gotta keep 'em in line or they'll do you."

The third man, Mack Childs, was a medical assistant at one of
the city's hospitals. He was a year or two older than her, with a shock
of unruly hair that seamlessly merged into his beard. He looked

suspicious and exhausted. "I looked in on Ezekiel Wallace this Tuesday past, yes. I don't normally do visits to The Phillips Suites, but their regular man was unwell, and I agreed to substitute for him. Mr. Wallace seemed in reasonable spirits, compared to many men his age. I helped him bone a chicken, and then tidied his kitchen and removed his garbage to the communal dump. His home was in good order otherwise. I didn't notice anyone who struck me as unusual, no, nor hear anything suspicious. I am tired, yes. It's been a long week so far."

Back at the Suites, Emma found Mr. Iver still in his office. He looked up at her approach, a mixture of emotions on his face.

"I have a suspicion as to who attacked the old man," she told him.

Who does Emma suspect?

HINT:

Detail.

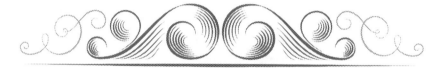

HOWARD'S END

The victim, Ryan Howard, had lived in a large, attractive house in one of the city's wealthier districts. Carpenter Road was one of the city's more expensive residential streets. For historical reasons, the houses were set in generous grounds, and the road was close enough to the heart of the city to be convenient, but far enough away to be quiet.

The road itself was unusually wide, and lined with old, attractive trees. Howard's property was at number twenty-three. Low, faux-rustic fencework separated it from the road, wound through with an assortment of vines and creepers carefully prevented from protruding outward. On the other three sides, Parnacki could see tall hedges in front of taller partition fences. There were several big old trees to the side of the house, moving on behind it. The man's children were grown now, but one of the trees still held an extensive treehouse, carefully designed to look simple and artless when you looked past the bark-brown metal safety cables and supporting struts.

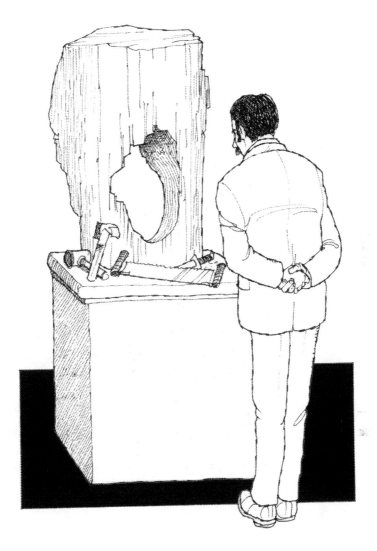

In front of the house, the folksy theme presented itself as a path from gate to door made from slices of raw tree trunk, heavily lacquered against the weather. Several pieces of large-scale wooden sculpture sat around the front, some part-finished. There was a significant array of tools arranged around them—a small, wicked hatchet with a six-inch blade, two adzes, a big old logging axe, a seven-inch hunter's knife with a sharply diamond-shaped hand guard, four chisels spread evenly in width from a palm to less than a finger, a hefty-looking hammer, a heavy saw with a clear sheen of oil, and something not dissimilar to an ice-pick, which had a stone handle. Clearly, the visitor was supposed to assume that Howard had become a keen and highly talented sculptor in his latter years.

Inside the house, all hint of rustic artifice vanished. The kitchen was aggressively modern, from the brushed steel chimney hood over the top-of-the-line stove to the sparkling ceramic tile floor. Even the

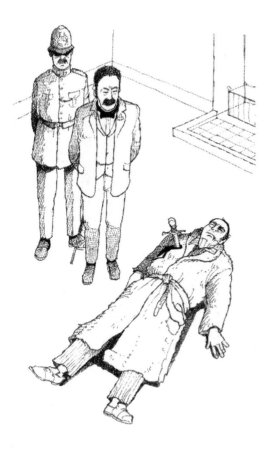

table and chairs in there were brass and chrome constructions, burnished to a shine. The reception room looked to have been ripped new from a seventeenth-century manor and carefully preserved down through the centuries. There was one piece of oriental porcelain, in particular, that had to be worth as much as a modest home.

The body was in the private office. It was a schizophrenic room, higgledy-piggledy with elements from the rest of the house and beyond— Chinoiserie, Nouveau,

Ruralism, even some stark functionality. It looked comfortable, however, which the other rooms had not. Sergeant Sullivan was in the office, examining the paperwork on the desk.

Howard's corpse was on the floor between the door and the fireplace, clad in a thick dressing gown, fleecy pyjama bottoms, and a pair of house slippers. He'd been killed by a clean stab to the chest, about two inches wide, which was surrounded by a straight-edged rhomboidal bruise mark. It was carefully placed between the fourth and fifth ribs. The left eye was surrounded by significant bruising, and there was a tear to the upper lip that suggested some sort of blow to the mouth as well.

Parnacki looked over at his sergeant. "Anything curious in the documents, Sullivan?"

"Nothing obviously out of order, sir," he said.

The Inspector nodded. "Very well. I've seen enough here. I'll take the likely murder weapon to the station, and examine the papers there."

Why does Parnacki believe that he has identified the murder weapon?

HINT:

Staging.

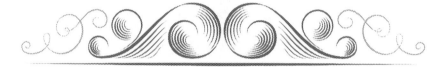

CARTWRIGHT

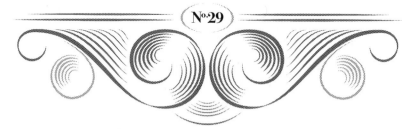

№·29

T he lady of Cartwright House, Mrs. Dionne Abouelela, was a mannerly woman. Emma had been in her supposed employ for ten days, and although she'd been assigned lighter duties, the period had been another reminder of the sheer drudgery of domestic work. In the time she'd been at Cartwright house, she'd gotten to cordial speaking terms with the staff, and had seen at least a dozen assorted members of the extended family.

Several expensive items had been stolen from Cartwright House in the previous six months—four of them from obscure corners of the property, making it difficult to precisely identify dates. The police, while keen to help, had been unable to make any headway, and Mrs. Abouelela was out of patience. So one of Emma's more surreptitious tasks was to survey the house at least four times a day, looking for thefts. Her visual memory made it a simple enough matter, but she still had to dust everything well enough to allay suspicions amongst the other staff.

It was afternoon on a warm, relentlessly blue-skied Saturday, and Emma was in the entertainments room when she realized that a small matchbox made of gold filigree inset with garnets was missing from its spot. She immediately made her way to the smaller reception room, where Mrs. Abouelela was entertaining a guest.

The woman looked up at her approach, her face carefully neutral. "Yes, girl?"

"Your tisane, madam," she said.

"I see." She paused, then turned to her guests. "Excuse me, will you? I'll only be a moment." She followed Emma out of the room and down the corridor a way, stopping by a small marble bust of Cicero. "You have news, Mrs. Warren?"

"Yes, ma'am. A gold matchbox, taken from beside the billiards table. It was there when I was last through just before lunch."

"You're sure?"

"Absolutely."

The woman frowned. "Then we finally have a shot at finding this light-fingered fool. How do you want to proceed?"

"Staff are always here to talk to, but visitors go home. We should speak with them first. It's Fanny, Alan, and Jasper today?"

"Yes, that's right. What approach will you take?"

"You must be the one to question them, of course," Emma said. "In your personal sitting room, I think. Speak to them one at a time, and tell them... Tell them a piece of glassware was broken, one of the figurines in the music room, and ask them where they've been since lunch, and if they happen to have noticed anything. I'll stand in the corner of the room and watch them very carefully. After that, I'll work through the house staff."

She nodded. "Very well."

A few minutes later, the pair were set up in Mrs. Abouelela's room. A quiet knock on the door heralded the butler's admission of her third son, Alan. He looked apprehensive as he entered, an expression that he typically wore in her presence, and when she asked him about his movements and observations, he blinked. "No, Mother, I didn't see or hear anything I'm afraid. I went for a stroll after lunch." He noticed his mother looking at a soggy shirt-cuff, and picked at it irresolutely. "I managed to get showered on, of course. I've only been back

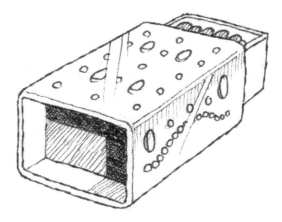

about quarter of an hour. Sorry I can't be of use."

Fanny, Alan's daughter, was tickled by the idea of a mysterious breakage. "I knew that talk of tisanes had to be bunk, Auntie Dee. It must be one of the maids, of course. Unless Jasper... Surely he'd be far too proper to touch, though. Does the housekeeper know where the staff were? But I suppose if she did, you wouldn't need to ask me! I didn't notice anything, but I was painting until we took tea, and it does get so absorbing. I say! You don't think it could have been old Gordon's ghost, do you?"

Jasper, the third visitor, was Fanny's brother. He was a somewhat stuffy young man, and took his dignity a deal too seriously. "My word, Aunt Dionne. That is most careless of the responsible party, and shocking that she might attempt to evade her responsibility. I regret that I am unable to assist in uncovering this individual. I have been in the library since lunch, but I did not hear any noise similar to a breakage, and I did not notice any particular members of staff. My apologies. You must be quite upset."

After he had left, Emma frowned. "I don't think we need to move onto the staff just yet, ma'am," she said.

Why does Emma suspect one of the visitors?

HINT:

Day.

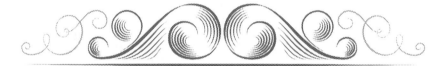

THE BOAT

I t had been three weeks since the tragic death of Anthony Block, and Leigh, his widow, was still trying to come to terms with the idea that he was gone. Her friends were reluctant to intrude, but concern had finally overpowered politesse, so Miss Miller and a couple of others resolved to pay the bereaved woman a call.

If Leigh was surprised to see her friends on the doorstep, she didn't show it. She looked at the trio listlessly. "Hello," she said.

"Leigh, my dear," Miss Miller said. "May we come in?"

"I suppose so." She stepped back from the doorway.

Miss Miller led the way through to the sitting room, and as Leigh filtered in, ushered her to her customary armchair.

Dinah Bagg, bringing up the rear, said, "I'll make some tea, shall I?"

"Good idea," said Netty Magner, as if the trio hadn't planned it out. "I'll give you a hand."

While Dinah checked the kitchen's food stocks and Netty went to make sure that clean clothes were available, Miss Miller sat on the settee near Leigh and patted her hand.

"I'm so sorry, Leigh," she said.

The other woman shrugged. "It's not your fault, Mary."

Miss Miller said nothing.

After a pause, Leigh shrugged again. "It's just one of those things, isn't it. Everyone knows that boats are dangerous in bad weather." She trailed off for a long moment, and then words were spilling out of her. "Everything feels like such a preposterous nightmare. Do you know? One minute they're cooling their heels in the cabin with a game of Ludo of all stupid things, and the next he's over the side and just gone. It was all they could find to play. I've heard that drowning is a peaceful way to die. I'd like to believe it, but it doesn't sound very peaceful to me. That horrible burning in your chest. It was Damian Johnson, of course. Any time Tony got into any mischief, it was always Damian behind it. Always had been, since they were boys. They reserved the boat a couple of months ago, and although the weather was said to be a bit unpleasant, they decided to go anyway. It's not as if fish were ever the point of fishing, for those two. So they went out, and sure as eggs are eggs, the wind picked up. Damian told me all about it, poor man. They pulled up their lines and went to shelter in the cabin when the waves picked up. They were being tossed around a lot, but it didn't worry them because the boat is a sturdy little thing. It gets taken out into the deep ocean sometimes, apparently. Do you know that the waves out there get almost like cliffs of water? But they were only a few miles off the coast. No danger of being smashed on any rocks. So they sat in there for a while, killing time and talking nonsense, I dare say, and then the wind suddenly died down. Tony always was excitable. He leapt up and went outside the cabin to have a look. The waves hadn't finished, though, and as he was at the rail, he was just . . . just... Then the winds rose again.

Just a respite, you see. Damian couldn't even get out to see if there was anything to be done. That was all there was to it. Tony was gone. Oh my God, Mary. He's gone." She dissolved into wracking sobs.

Miss Miller put her arms around the woman, and the other two quickly came forward to join her.

Some time later, Miss Miller took Dinah to one side, leaving Leigh in Netty's company. "I refuse to burden Leigh any further, so not a word to her, Dinah. You understand? We absolutely need to discover why Damian is lying about Anthony's death."

Why does Miss Miller think Damian Johnson is lying?

HINT:

Waves.

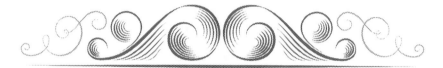

THE WAREHOUSE

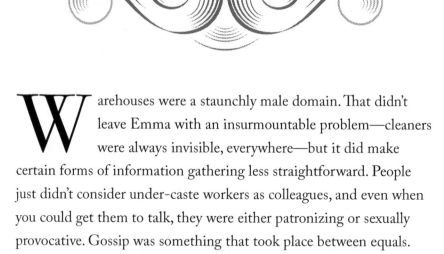

№ 31

Warehouses were a staunchly male domain. That didn't leave Emma with an insurmountable problem—cleaners were always invisible, everywhere—but it did make certain forms of information gathering less straightforward. People just didn't consider under-caste workers as colleagues, and even when you could get them to talk, they were either patronizing or sexually provocative. Gossip was something that took place between equals.

Baxter Brothers sold engine parts, some of them small and intricate enough to be worth stealing. Thefts were an occasional problem for them, but this time the light-fingered employee was proving unusually evasive. Deliveries came from and went to places all over the region and even beyond, so the warehouse ran all day and night, and boasted a prominent clock on the wall to attest to the fact, with shift times marked on the face.

The most common time for mischief in a twenty-four hour site was around 4 am, when watchful eyes were sleepiest. So Emma had been pushing a broom around the warehouse on the graveyard shift for four days, and wasn't in the best of moods. Twenty minutes earlier, around eight thirty, one of the morning arrivals had somehow dropped a container of thick, greasy soup all over a packing machine. She'd managed to get the device working again, but it was leaving marks on the packages, and the morning's supervisor was determined that it was her problem to fix.

It took her another quarter of an hour of back-breaking contortion to scrub the grease off the machine's cylinders. When she finally extracted herself, she discovered that half the shift were gathered around, smirkingly watching her. She forced herself to smile, dropped them a sarcastic little curtsey, and stalked off before she did something unprofessional.

A moment later, a junior clerk appeared,

and told her the manager wanted to see her.

David Underwood was a thin, wide-eyed man in his early thirties, a young enough manager that Emma assumed a father or uncle had put him in the role. Whether that was true or not, he was not a secure man, and he expressed his doubts in aggression. He leapt to his feet as she entered the office, and thumped his fist into his other palm.

"This is intolerable," he said, not quite shouting. "You've been here for days, Mrs. Warren. Very expensive days. And you've done absolutely nothing. Nothing!" His voice rose an octave. "And now we've lost more stock! Is this some sort of joke? Are you laughing at me, woman?"

Emma's patience collapsed, and her eyes narrowed. "Yes."

He stared at her, spluttering and turning purple.

Before he could start up again, she walked up close to him, dug her fingers into his shoulder firmly enough to be uncomfortable, and pushed him down into his chair. "I am not your wife or your daughter or your minion, Mr. Underwood," she said, her words icily sharp. "I am not a safe person to bully. Attempt to physically intimidate me again, and I will break you. If you cannot be civil, I will abandon you to your thief, and my employer will congratulate me, and pass around word that you are a pariah. Do we understand each other?"

"I... How dare..."

She stared at him coldly. "Do. We. Understand. Each. Other?"

Underwood shrank in on himself. "Yes, Mrs. Warren."

"That's nice," she said. "Now, why don't you tell me what has happened?"

He glowered at her, then sighed. "There was another theft from the secure room last night. Right under—that is, between the watchman's patrols at two forty and two fifty." He glanced at the carriage clock on his desk. "Less than six hours ago. The foreman was on the warehouse floor continually from midnight to 6 am, supervising the men under him, and he logged their movements carefully. One of them was home ill, but of the three remaining, one took his break from ten past two to two thirty, another from three to three twenty, and the last worked through in order to leave a little early. There was no one else here. The foreman would have seen any outsider trying to sneak in. The watchman is beyond reproach. The men were all clearly on the floor, working." He paused. "It's extraordinarily frustrating."

"Really?" Emma asked, her face as innocent as she could make it. "The culprit is obvious."

Why does Emma say that the thief's identity is obvious?

HINT:

Opportunity.

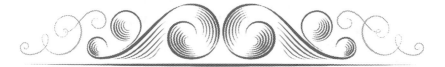

THE BANKER

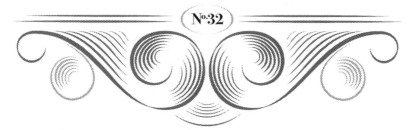

N°32

T here was no doubt that Damian Johnson had been an unpleasant man. He'd been arrested for violent outbursts a couple of times, and he'd put his wife in the hospital more than once. She was there again, in fact, following a savage beating the day before his death, and remained unresponsive thirty-six hours later. The list of potential killers was long, and plausibly included most of the staff at the victim's bank. Given the precarious state of their mother, though, the man's sons were Inspector Parnacki's leading suspects.

Johnson had been killed in his drawing-room, stabbed repeatedly through the neck. He'd died on the floor of the room in a large pool of blood. The murderer had watched him die, standing over the corpse long enough to leave a clear boot-print, size eight, in the puddle. The murder weapon, abandoned in the corpse, was a kitchen knife of a brand common enough that it could have been taken from half the homes in the city.

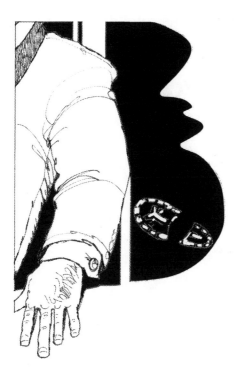

Other than the murder itself, there seemed to be nothing out of place in the victim's home. No items appeared to have been stolen, there were no signs of any significant struggle, and no evidence of anything having been ransacked. The victim's wallet remained on him. Some of the items in the room appeared to be of notable financial value, chief among them a weighty gold coin from the sixteenth century in a display case.

Having examined the murder scene closely, Parnacki moved on to the bank that the victim had managed. All three of his sons worked there, but so did forty-odd other people who had no reason to love the man. The Inspector found the three sons huddled in an unhappy, tired knot in their father's office.

As he entered, they all looked up, and one, somewhat older-looking, stepped forward. "You are here about Father's death," he said. "The cleaner informed us earlier."

The cleaner seemed likely to be the victim's housekeeper, Mrs. Lambert, who had initially reported the murder. "Yes. Inspector Parnacki, at your service. I'm sorry for your loss."

"Mark Johnson. Matt, Luke and I were together last night. We visited Mother, and then went together to Luke's, where we shared a bottle of Scotch, played cards poorly, and fretted about Mother. We haven't slept."

The other two men nodded gravely.

Parnacki examined the trio carefully. The middle brother, Matt, had a slender build compared to the other two, with smallish feet, a size six. He looked close in age to Mark, who was taller and heavier built, and who looked to wear a size eleven. Luke was clearly younger, perhaps only in his mid-twenties, but he was cut from the same cloth as Mark, and took a similar shoe. "I see," he said finally. "Do you know of anyone who might have wanted to hurt your father?"

Luke laughed bitterly. "He was an angry, impatient man who believed that other people were put on Earth to serve him."

Matt nodded, his eyes hard.

"Father antagonized plenty of people," Mark said, his voice firm. "And he received many threats over the years."

"As you sow," Luke said.

"Be that as it may," Parnacki said, "murder has consequences, and we all know which one of you is under arrest for the killing of your father."

Which brother does Parnacki suspect of being the murderer?

HINT:

Possibilities.

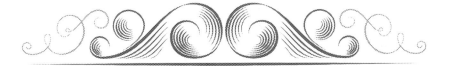

HATCHARDS

Nº 33

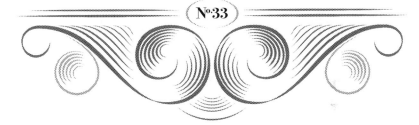

When he wasn't engaged in bird-watching, Oswald Ware was the general manager of Hatchards, a firm that made navigational instruments and other such systems for the maritime industry. He was a pleasant, congenial man, and it was an agreeable surprise when he appeared at Miss Miller's door without notice.

Once he was seated comfortably and Lucy, the maid, had duly furnished the pair of them with tea and a selection of biscuits, and after Aubrey, her calico cat, had taken his fill of winding around both their ankles, she decided it was time to put Oswald out of his obvious discomfort.

"Something is the matter, Oswald. Please, just come out with it."

He chuckled half-heartedly. "I'm transparent, it seems. Yes, I have a problem, and after your incredible work retrieving Leona's stolen china, I very much hoped I might prevail on your assistance."

"Always, my dear."

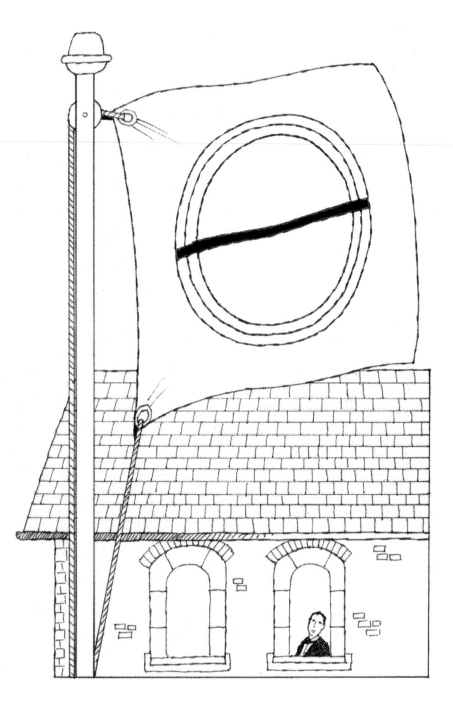

"Well. Thank you. Yesterday, a set of ledgers and client books were stolen from the office safe. I was only out of the room for fifteen minutes that afternoon between two and two fifteen. The materials were there before lunchtime, but not at close. It had to have been whilst I was away. It's hard to think, but only my assistant managers have keys and the combination. If they... Well. It could quite easily ruin Hatchards. I was hoping you could speak to them quietly, perhaps tomorrow?"

She smiled. "I will certainly do my best."

So the next morning, Miss Miller found herself walking through the impressive wrought-iron Hatchards gates. The name was written in huge decorative scrollwork letters above the gates, whilst the company's logo—three plain concentric circles, horizontally bisected with a heavy line—appeared repeatedly in the gates' design. This simple logo also appeared on the side of the main warehouse, as a large rectangular flag atop a tall flagpole, and masquerading as a cunningly worked weather vane on the roof. It was all very imposing, undoubtedly.

As she made her way through the courtyard toward the main door, Oswald appeared. He was effusively grateful, and escorted her through the building to his office, a large room which housed not only his own desk and accoutrements, but also the desks of all four of his assistant managers. The safe, two feet square, was set into the wall behind Oswald's desk. A glass door at one end of the room led to a smaller, more luxurious meeting room, where he offered her a seat.

"Well. How should we proceed, Mary?"

She considered it a moment. "I think we want them a little unsettled. Stay at your desk. Explain nothing. Tell them only that they should answer my questions as fully as possible, give them instructions to keep silent before and after meeting with me, and then send them in to me one at a time. Come back after them."

"As you say," he said. "The first will be in momentarily."

The first fellow in was tall, dignified, and impeccably tailored. If the events unsettled him at all, he hid it well.

"I am Miss Miller," she told him. "Please be seated. I have a few questions."

"Delighted to meet you," he said pleasantly. "Andrew MacLean-Finney."

She nodded. "What is your role at Hatchards, Mr. MacLean-Finney?"

"Assistant manager in charge of after-sales. I make sure our customers are happy, and keep them provisioned with consumables, replacements, new units, and the such."

"Were you in the office yesterday afternoon between two and two fifteen?"

"Yes, I was back by then—wait, no, actually. I got to the office about one thirty. I'd been here for half an hour or so when I glanced out and noticed that the company flag was upside down, so I went to have it corrected. I checked the time when I got back, and it was two twelve."

"Thank you," Miss Miller told him. "That will be all for now."

The next fellow in, Garfield Barrett, was a dashing forty-something who was responsible for new sales. "I'm afraid I wasn't, no," he told her. "I had a prospective client here, and I was showing him around. At two, I'd just handed him to the factory foreman for ten minutes, while I made sure that the warehouse was in good order."

Charles Gay was the assistant manager of operations. He was in his fifties, of medium height and build, with a shrewd light in his eyes. "Two, you say? Hm. No, not at my desk, actually. The chief engineer

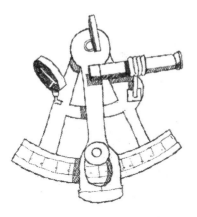

has been having some issues with one of the machines. He's a tricky guy to track down, always being called hither and thither, you understand. So I was having a little hunt for him. Found him in the casings room in the end, fixing some widget or other. That was about ten past two. We were another twenty or so talking."

The last of the four, Lawrence Waters, was a small, slender, tired-looking man in his late thirties. He was the assistant manager of financial affairs. "Mr. Ware left the office at two on the dot. I followed him out, and made my way to the break room. I brewed myself a strong mug of coffee, and spent a few minutes quietly consuming it. I returned at precisely thirteen minutes past. Andrew was there, and Mr. Ware returned three minutes after that."

After the interviews were done, Oswald returned, looking cautiously optimistic. "Any luck?"

"I'm almost completely certain of your thief's identity. You should get into place, barring the office door," she told him. "We don't want him bolting for it."

Who does Miss Miller suspect, and why?

HINT:

Reasons.

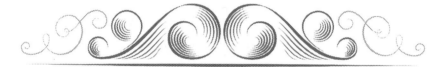

GET CARTER

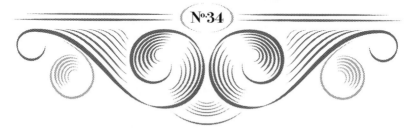

Nº 34

Emma Warren had been investigating Ricky Carter for three days. Knight and Sons was a huge operation employing well over a hundred people to produce a wide range of metallic bits and pieces to a host of different industries. Pilfering was an endemic problem, but there was a larger ongoing issue of systematic theft. Ross Knight, the head of the company, had recently become quite sure that Carter was responsible, but rather than dismiss the man, he wanted evidence he could take to the police.

Looking into the man, she'd come up against a lot of resistance from other staff. People were wary of gossiping about him. Given that he was a balding lecher with absolutely frightful teeth, that had been something of a surprise, and certainly suggested that Ross Knight was on the right track with his suspicions.

One woman, a late-shift cleaner named Patience, had confirmed that the man was well known as someone for women only to approach in groups. Even she wouldn't say much more than that, though. His conduct was clearly beyond the pale, and his position in the company was quite lowly, so it seemed a little odd that he hadn't been fired years ago.

Over the days, Emma had put together the beginnings of a solid log of suspicious actions and disturbing anecdotes. She had been confident that it was just a matter of a few more days before there was enough to pass to a police investigation.

Now, Ricky Carter was dead.

His body had been found at the lathe he manned. Emma stood near it with Ross Knight, looking at the scene. A piece of the machinery looked to have come loose as he sat there working, spiking out to stab him through the upper thigh before retracting. He'd managed to get out of his seat inside the machine and stagger a few steps before collapsing, stretched out. From the prodigious pool of blood, his death had been quick.

The loose piston was quite obvious, hanging in an obtrusive position over the operator's seat, still blood-smeared for about six

inches of its length. It was a sharp-
ended piece of metal about an inch
and a half in diameter, a perfect
match to the hole punched through
Carter's trousers and into the leg

beneath. The man's last expression had been one of horror, fittingly
enough.

It perhaps wasn't strange that no one had noticed the accident
happening—he'd been on an early shift, and his machine was at the
end of a row with few other people around. But his death must have
come quickly indeed to prevent him from crying out audibly for
assistance.

Knight's face bore a curious mix of disgust and relief as he looked
at the corpse, a sentiment that would probably be echoed by all the
women working for the firm, as well as many of the men. After a
minute, he turned to Emma and gave her an apologetic look. "I
suppose that this means we will no longer require your services, Mrs.
Warren."

She nodded. "Yes, I'm afraid that the police need to take over at this
point."

He blinked at her. "The police?"

"Mr. Knight, I'm afraid that Ricky Carter was murdered, and
probably because I started investigating him."

Why does Emma think that Carter was murdered?

HINT:

Corpse.

THE MASK

N⁰35

It was always somewhat disconcerting to wake up in an unfamiliar bedroom. Miss Miller blinked once or twice at the powder-blue runner near the top of the wall before her memory reconnected fully with her consciousness. She was staying at Banhurst, her cousin Amelia's expansive semi-rural estate. It was her first time sleeping in the Viennese Room, and the bed was a little too soft, but there were a number of excellent pieces in the room's cabinets.

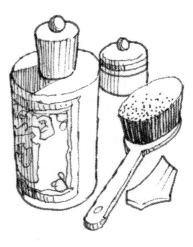

Permitting herself a yawn and a stretch, she swung herself upright and glanced out of the window. It promised to be a fine day, and bright sunshine always highlighted the sight of birds' feathers delightfully. She'd left her overnight bag at the foot of the room's ornate display case. She looked into it, confirming that her toiletry pouch was at the top. She frowned slightly at a small sliver of glass sitting on it and reminded herself to ensure she kept the bag closed, then pulled her toiletries out and began the process of getting herself fit and ready.

After a long, pleasant breakfast with Amelia in the small dining room—something of a misnomer, given it could comfortably seat a dozen—Miss Miller set out into the grounds, armed with her notebooks and binoculars. Her cousin sometimes joined her, but not on this occasion. Her husband, a leading politician in his own right, was hosting a significant dinner party that evening. Preparations could become quite complex when one entertained the powerful.

She returned to Banhurst at lunchtime in very high spirits. She'd spotted a pair of particularly uncommon warblers, and had managed to make copious notes and a few sketches before they moved on. All in all, it had been a very pleasant retreat. The previous evening had been exquisite—Mrs. Shaw had been testing recipes for the dinner party, and had surpassed herself—and Amelia had been on very good form throughout.

Lunch was a little more hurried than breakfast had been. Amelia's advice was required for an innumerable train of small decisions, and it was clear she was distracted. As the ladies were finishing their salmon, the interruptions ebbed.

"Mary, my dear," Amelia said, "did you happen to notice a delicate crystal mask

of Mozart's face in your room?" She
paused, and grimaced. "In a cabinet, of
course. Not floating around the place or
anything ghastly."

Miss Miller thought back. "I don't
recall it," she said. "But delightful as
the room is, I'm ashamed to admit that
I didn't spend much time on the art in
there."

"Ah, well."

"Is something the matter with it,
Amelia?"

"In a sense. I popped up there to check that the girl hadn't left
any of your things when she brought your bag down, and it's missing.
There's been a lot of staff in and out of that room in the last day or
so, though. One maid cleaned and aired it out yesterday morning, the
coachman took your bag up in the afternoon, another maid made the
bed while we were at dinner, and then one of tonight's extras brought
your bag down again. Any one of them might have made away with it,
I suppose."

Miss Miller pondered that for a moment. "Actually, I doubt anyone
stole it, but I suspect I can tell you who knows for sure."

Why does Miss Miller think she knows what happened to the mask?

HINT:

Timing.

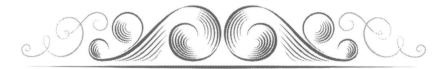

McDOWELL

The victim, Elliott McDowell, had telephoned into the police station the previous evening to report an attack that later became his own murder. The transcript included in his case file made for unpleasant reading.

"I've... Please send help. Fast. I was attacked... A man, he had a knife. Wanted money. I don't . . . don't know how he got in. He stabbed me. He had a knife. It's bad. I... The clock... I must have passed out. Half an hour ago. 8.20. I'm very cold. The wound is still... I'm still bleeding. Please. Number Twelve. Lynwood Gardens. Hurry."

Inspector Parnacki moved from the transcript to the responding officers' report. Police and medical assistance got to the house ten minutes later, but it wasn't fast enough. The man was dead. They found him in his study, slumped on the floor. He had gotten blood all over himself—hair, face, hands, arms and legs—and the clothing around the wound in his stomach was soaked through. More blood was pooled around him where he lay. Other than that, the room was spotless. Likewise, the only signs of disorder in the room were that the telephone's earpiece lay on the desk, and a couple of desk drawers had obviously been searched. McDowell had clearly been a neat person.

He'd been in his forties, a successful financier. He did not appear to have any professional rivals, but he had in the last year married a woman twenty years his junior, named Judith Burke. The marriage appeared happy, according to nearby residents the investigating sergeant had spoken to. Two months ago, however, the couple had reported an unpleasant incident with one of Mrs. McDowell's former admirers, a man named Dean Williams. The lady herself was currently visiting grandparents some three hundred miles away, and efforts were being made to contact her. Williams had agreed to come in for questioning, and was in the process of being settled.

Financiers tended to accrue enemies only if they bankrupted firms or investors, and according to McDowell's secretary, he had done neither in the last few years. His work was cautious by the standards of the trade, and there was no evidence of his having earned any particular wrath professionally.

Sergeant Sullivan knocked on Parnacki's door. "Mr. Williams is ready for you in Room 2, Inspector."

Parnacki nodded, and went to speak to the fellow.

Dean Williams was in his early thirties, a handsome man with slightly unruly brown hair, glittering eyes, and a ready smile. "I'm a fitter," he told the Inspector. "I specialize, if that's the word, in ceramic floor tiling, but I've done it all in my time: carpeting, wainscoting, parquet, cupboards, whatever anyone needs done. That's how I met Jude—fixing up her father's front hall. We hit it off immediately, but I never forgot that she was quality. So no, I never had any long-term designs on her. No realistic ones, anyway. We snuck around for a bit, which was wonderful, but I always knew she'd marry a professional. Yes, I did make a fool of myself once a couple of months ago. Her new place is only a couple of miles from mine. I'd been drinking and got to feeling maudlin, and yes, I called her husband some unpleasant things—but I apologized once I sobered up, and it won't happen again. Eight twenty last night? Last night was cribbage night. I was at my local, the Raven, from six to eight thirty. We lost, against the idiots from the Old White Hart. Dozens of people will confirm that for you. Afterwards, I called it a night and went home to bed."

Parnacki nodded. "Mr. Williams, I'm arresting you on suspicion of the murder of Elliott McDowell."

Why does Parnacki think Williams can be the murderer?

HINT:

File.

RIVERSIDE

№·37

Miss Miller was heading into the warrens of Riverside, the Weblin family home, when one of the maids, a girl named Cora, appeared from a side passage. The girl shied back to avoid bumping into her, and turned her momentary confusion into a quick curtsey. "Oh! Hello ma'am. Can I help you?" she asked. She rubbed her damp hands on her apron briskly.

"Cora, isn't it?" Miss Miller asked. "I'm fine, thank you. Squires told me that Sophia is in the kitchen. I know the way."

The girl nodded and smiled. "Right you are, ma'am. I'm headed back that way myself. Just washing my hands." She fell in a polite step behind Miss Miller.

"How's the day treating you so far, Cora?"

"Mustn't grumble, ma'am. Cook's preparing a steak pudding for dinner, so there's suet to be grated up and dough to be rolled out. I like that better than slicing onions."

"Yes, I can imagine. Mrs. Crews is quite the expert in her cookery."

"I'm learning an awful lot from her, ma'am. She's a dab hand, and no mistake."

They turned into the large kitchen. Mrs. Crews glanced up from the table where Sophia was talking to her, and shot Cora a miniscule frown. The girl curtseyed again, and darted past an impressive row of sinks and basins to a stove, where what looked like stock was simmering away.

"Mary!" Sophia smiled broadly. "How lovely to see you. I hope to be able to show you a treat outside. Mrs. C., I'll go over Thursday and Friday with you later."

"Very well, madam," the cook said. "Should I prepare some tea?"

"That would be lovely," Sophia said. "We'll be near the croquet lawn, so serving it there will be fine."

"Of course, madam. Cora, kettle!"

Mary followed Sophia out through the door and into the herb garden. "There's been a wonderful assortment of finches in the nut trees this last month," the woman said. "I do so hope they put on a good show for you this morning."

"All we can ever do is give them the opportunity," Miss Miller said. "How are you, my dear?"

"Oh, well enough, thank you. I'll be at the Society's monthly presentation next week for sure. Things are always a little busy this time of year. You know how Patrick is about his golf."

Miss Miller smiled. "Indeed, I do. Always seemed like a waste of a perfectly lovely walk to me, smashing those little balls around the countryside. I'm sure he's equally baffled by birding, of course."

"Quite. He loves being out in the countryside, but he can't quite bring himself to do it unless there's a clear purpose being served. Even if that purpose is just friendly competition."

They were approaching the nasturtium border that marked out the croquet lawn. Miss Miller paused a moment. "Sophia, forgive me if I'm prying, but is everything well with the house?"

The other woman stopped and turned to look at her, an eyebrow raised. "I've heard the gossip. 'Mary Miller can work wonders,' that sort of thing. There *have* been some thefts of the last few months, as it happens. Money, mostly. Are you some sort of spiritualist medium or something?"

Miss Miller permitted herself a small smile. "Most people don't take the time to properly observe their surroundings and their fellows, that's all. It's perfectly natural. The familiar is difficult for the mind to really sink its teeth into. I just happen to notice details. Have you considered Cora, the kitchen maid, as your pilferer?"

Why is Miss Miller suspicious of Cora?

HINT:

Actions.

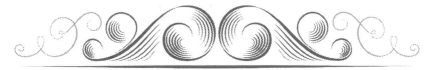

THE INDUSTRIAL MUSEUM

Nº38

J eremiah Drabwell was a man who lived up to his name. A
fussy fellow of middling height and build, he dressed in
smartly dull clothing and spoke in a slightly nasal voice with
the sort of pontificating manner that Emma typically associated
with boring vicars. He was undoubtedly fantastically intelligent and
knowledgeable, but it was probably for the best that his role as director
kept him away from the museum's actual visitors.

"We have, simply, brought together the world's largest and most
important collection of clockwork mechanisms for this exhibition,
Mrs. Warren. It is a superlative trust that has been placed in us by
all manner of institutions, and it must not be permitted to falter. I
have been credibly warned that there is going to be an attempt to
steal one or more of the smaller, more valuable mechanisms in our
care over the course of this coming week. All my staff are on high

alert. I have every faith in them. 'Measure twice and cut once,' is the path of prudence, however, and thus your presence here. Be vigilant." Drabwell rattled to a stop.

Emma blinked, and quickly scanned her memory of the lecture. "Yes, sir. You can rely on me."

He nodded seriously, then turned and toddled away with no further comment.

Two afternoons later, she was amongst the staff at the main doors. It was a weekday, so foot traffic was reasonably light. A knot of eight made up mostly of students, family types, and retirees were gathered together for one of the guided tour sessions. One bored, over-dressed young woman was amongst the group. Emma watched as she deliberately flicked her mane of hair at a peg-legged old fellow on crutches, then smiled false apologies at him. The guide spotted it, and hurried them all into moving off, slowing his pace significantly so the old man could keep up.

As they were rounding the corner, a pair of tall, burly men in dark suits and long overcoats came through the doors. One had brown hair, and appeared in his thirties. The other was a little older, and had dark hair that was starting to recede. They scanned the room before stepping forward to get their entry stamps and move into the museum. Drabwell appeared at her elbow. "Please keep an eye on those gentlemen, Mrs. Warren," he said quietly.

She nodded. "Of course."

There was a clipboard on the desk next to her for the specific purpose of helping her be less noticeable around the museum. She picked it up, and set off behind the suited men. They seemed in no particular hurry, so she meandered behind them, moving from exhibit to exhibit and making meaningless marks on a densely

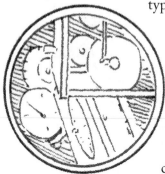

typed piece of paper. They moved in an odd pattern, she swiftly realized—spending around two and a half minutes on each exhibit, and leapfrogging each other every time, so that each man saw just half of the displays.

They'd just got to some of the twelfth-century displays when the museum's fire bell started shrieking its alert. Emma realized that there was indeed a faint tang of smoke in the air. She moved toward the entrance hall immediately, still trying to watch as much as she could. The men also headed in the same direction, strolling casually, side by side, as if out for a companionable walk. Other staff and visitors began to appear, moving with clear urgency. The tour group ran out of a side room, without the guide. The over-dressed woman was in the lead, eyes wide with panic, making loud whimpering noises. The other seven were close behind her, and the group tore past the suited men. Behind them, back down the hallway, Emma could hear their guide's annoyed calls for calm.

Blinking, Emma grabbed her radio. "Barricade the doors, sir," she barked. "Right now. I know who the thief is."

Who does Emma suspect of being the thief?

HINT:

Movements.

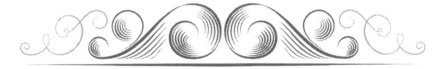

PELTON STREET

№39

osemary Ellis had been dead for five days before the paperboy noticed his daily newspapers piling up in the hall and thought to mention it to one of her nearby residents. She, in turn, tried the old woman's doorbell a few times over the course of the day, before contacting the police. Mrs. Ellis's death was confirmed late that night, after local constables forced the lock on the front door and found her body inside the kitchen. Although decomposition was progressing, there were suggestions of violence at the scene, which was why Inspector Parnacki found himself outside Number 35, Pelton Street at half past six in the morning.

The sun was barely up. Although the only open sign of life was the milkman's cart receding up the street, the Inspector could feel a number of eyes on him. Curtains were most definitely twitching. Number 35 was architecturally identical to all the other homes on the road, squat and semi-detached, two floors of brick topped with a slate roof. The beige curtains were firmly closed. A thin alley ran between

it and Number 33, bisected by a solid fence. A concrete path led from the front gate to a red wooden door, and a patch of thin lawn lurked behind some simple wooden trellis. There was nothing else there to give any impression of the occupant or hint at homeliness, not even a lawn ornament or a plant on a windowsill.

The other buildings up and down the street were cut from the same cloth, but most of the occupants had made efforts to brighten up their homes. Many front lawns boasted flowerbeds along the edges, and clotheslines were common, both empty and full. Some had hanging flower baskets on the eaves, or badly painted ornamental figures. Milk bottles sat outside almost every house, adding a hint of domesticity. One place even had a croquet area set up, with mallets sitting patiently in the grass. The clear sense of life going on gave Number 35 a stark, unhappy air.

The constable who'd been guarding the scene let him in to the house. It seemed much the same on the inside—clean, but lacking in character. The downstairs living room was mostly beige, like the curtains and the carpet. The furnishings looked old, albeit in good shape. The kitchen was similarly bland—wood and tile and porcelain without any real sense the person who used it. It made the disorder all the more striking. The table had been pushed back hard, enough that one of its chairs now lay underneath it, and a second was tilted at a crazy angle. A shattered mess of pottery and rotting fruit in a corner next to the stinking icebox had presumably been a fruit bowl at one point. A few bits of paper were scattered across the floor, small standing-order delivery invoices for bread, ice, milk, and newspaper, one of each a day. Another chair was by the back wall, near the door, one of the legs splintered clean off.

Parnacki looked around thoughtfully, then turned to the constable.

"Anything useful from the
nearby residents?"

"The deceased wasn't
popular, sir. Couldn't find
anyone to say a good word
about her, I couldn't. Next
door described her as pompous
and mean-spirited, and said
she never had any visitors.
She did tell me, though, that
the deceased had a daughter,
who she thought to be long-
estranged and now living with
her family on the other side of the country. None of the nearby
residents saw or heard any disturbance over the last week or so. No one
had the slightest inkling she was dead, apart from him what done it, if
it was actually foul play."

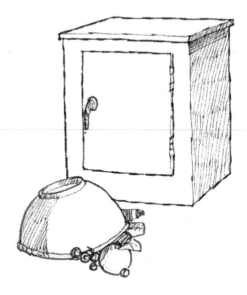

"One person knew," Parnacki said. "It doesn't mean he had anything
to do with it, but I think we should have a word."

*Why does Parnacki say that there was someone who knew about Mrs. Ellis's
death?*

HINT:

Absence.

LEVEL TWO

PUZZLES

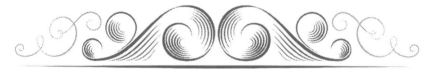

THE PASTORAL CARVING

N°·40

I f Ezekiel Mendez was not a regular attendee at Ornithological Society events, it was only that he rarely took evenings or weekends off from his work. He owned and operated a chain of dealerships in antiquities and objets d'art, and spent the great bulk of his time scrutinizing and negotiating purchases. The expertise that he'd gained made him an interesting conversationalist, and he'd always been perfectly pleasant. Miss Miller did not know him especially well, however, so his request to meet him for tea one afternoon at the Regal

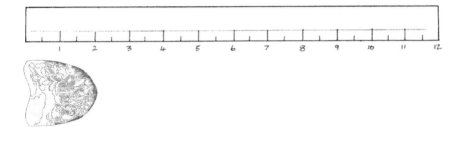

Hotel had certainly piqued her curiosity.

He arrived precisely on time, entering the Hotel's salon on the very stroke of four pm. Smiling warmly, he crossed over to the table Miss Miller had chosen, and sat.

"Mary, thank you for coming," he said. "I hope I haven't kept you waiting."

"Not at all," she said.

"Shall we spend a while exchanging pleasantries before I confess my reasons, or would you rather cut to the heart of the matter?"

She smiled. "I'm already intrigued, Ezekiel. I won't hold you hostage to propriety. We can catch up afterwards, if you have the time."

"As generous as ever. Thank you. The truth is, something of mine has been stolen, and I am very keen to get it back."

"You've tried the police," she said, making it a statement.

"Indeed. They're convinced that it's one of their usual suspects, and the piece will turn up in due course."

"You are less convinced."

Mendez nodded. "Just five other people in the country knew of its existence or location. The police insist that word must have spread, but the theft was too precise. It is one of my prospective clients—all of whom are wealthy and well regarded. I'm not surprised the police are in denial."

"Yes, I see. Perhaps you'd better start at the beginning."

"Thank you. On the 3rd, I returned from my biennial trip to Japan. I acquired a number of exciting items while I was there, but the prize was a very fine carved toggle, of a type called *netsuke*, from the early Edo period. It's small, no more than two inches in any dimension, carved from narwhal ivory in the shape of a heart. It is an exquisite piece, featuring an incredibly detailed pastoral scene. That alone would be noteworthy, but the piece is also a small puzzle-box—slide one branch a little, press on a particular cloud, then twist, and it pops open to reveal a tiny compartment." He paused. "I have never seen its like."

"It sounds magnificent," Miss Miller said.

"Very much so. I started making discreet inquiries as soon as I got back, and yesterday afternoon I held a viewing for five interested parties. That was at 5 pm. The *netsuke* was in my office at 7 pm, when I was suddenly called to an urgent meeting, and gone at 7.45 pm, when I returned. My idea now is to invite the five to lawn cocktails

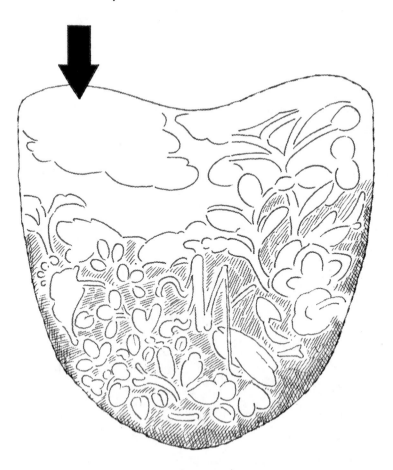

tomorrow afternoon, along with your good self and a number of others for cover. It is short notice, but I will word my invitations carefully, and the four innocents will most certainly turn up. All were very keen to stay in the running for the *netsuke*. The thief will be aware of this, and so will have to turn up as well. During the bash, perhaps you could find some suitably innocuous way to inquire as to their locations on Thursday evening, and see if something rouses your hackles."

Miss Miller frowned thoughtfully. "Hmm. Yes, that might work. The university's art institute held a short lecture on the Romantics yesterday evening, followed by a display borrowed from the museum. Just the sort of thing that one could gush about in a slightly tiresome manner. But your thief is bound to be on guard, and I can hardly demand answers if someone demurs."

"I understand completely," Mendez said. "All we can do is try. Thank you."

The following afternoon, armed with a tall glass of iced tonic water, Miss Miller surveyed the small crowd of guests from the edge of the statue garden that bordered Mendez's main lawn. His five suspects were all present and showing every appearance of pleasure. When an eddy in the conversational mingle around one them appeared, she moved in to pursue her chosen line of attack.

Her first suspect was George Wallis, a dashing young man in his thirties. The youngest son of a very wealthy dynasty, he had a reputation as a socialite and dilettante. "Oh yes," he said, when he introduced herself. "Of course! The esteemed Miss Miller, leading light of the Ornithological Society."

"I'd hardly call myself a leading light," she said.

"You're far too modest. How are you enjoying the afternoon? I didn't know you knew Zeke. Are you a collector?"

"Occasionally. But Mr. Mendez is also an occasional birder."

"Oh, I say! What fun." He leaned forward conspiratorially. "Any interesting feathered friends around this afternoon?"

"The party is a little loud for them, it seems. Perhaps later." She feigned a moment of uncertainty. "Didn't I spot you at the Institute's Romantics session on Thursday evening? Fascinating, wasn't it?"

"Alas, 'twas not me," Wallis said. "Perhaps foolishly, I agreed to take a role in the Revival Harlequinade at the Horizon Playhouse. I play Pantaloon himself! The newspapers have been awfully kind about my prancing around. It's a very merry time, but it does mean that I've not had a free evening all week. We're on next week, too. Just say the word if you're going to drop by, and I'll make sure you get a box. Curtains up at six thirty."

She thanked him and moved on.

The next prospect was Ross McKnight, an aging cattle baron and keen philanthropist, provided that the good causes in question were either orchestras or the very exclusive school his grandsons attended. He'd been a great beauty in his youth, but the years had revealed the truth of his measure, and he now looked like nothing so much as a grandiosely moustachioed weasel. He was polite, however, in a disinterested sort of way. "You're mistaken, I fear. I was dining with Demetrius Cabrera at the Empire. The European conductor, yes. He's doing a season at the Phil. A spectacular talent."

Penelope Finley was the wife of James Finley, who was a big name in the oil world. Miss Miller had met her at a number of previous events, and had found her to be a little flighty, if wilful. It took the best part of ten minutes to get her round to her activities on Thursday. "Oh, the night was so lovely, Mary. You should have seen it. Out on Lake Cloud, just James and I, the shore just a low glimmer and not a city twinkle to be seen. It's an experience not to be missed. The name? Oh yes, you must try it! The Waterlight. The very finest French cooking, a wonderful sommelier, excellent musicians, properly obedient and attentive waiters, and the stars open above you like a canopy. We reserved the whole restaurant, of course. So much more conducive that way."

Marcellus Koehler was a banker. Miss Miller had never heard of him before, but Mendez had described him as a quiet, professional sort of man, one who had no particular care for society or its antics. He was in his forties, smartly average in his appearance, and he seemed quite relieved to learn that she was an ornithologist. "Birds are a passion I can understand," he said. "Fascinating creatures, endlessly varied and deceptively clever. I'm not an outdoor type myself, but yes, I can see the appeal. I collect Orientalia, but the overlap—observation, patience, research, a private sort of satisfaction—is quite undeniable. Thursday? Not really my sort of thing, honestly. Occidental art is so . . . realistic. I prefer nuance. But let's see. I had a meeting with our host, then went to meet my delegation from Deutsche Bank. I am keeping them decently fed and entertained while they are in the city." In all, she and Koehler chatted for about half an hour, and she left his company feeling considerably less dour about Ezekiel Mendez's party.

The last suspect, Mitchell Lowe, was a very familiar face. One of the city's most outspoken judges, he seemed forever in the news for his radical opinions and harsh sentences. He had a small cloud of hangers-on around him at all times, dutifully tittering at his quips and soaking up his shockingly indiscreet stories. Miss Miller slipped into the group, and waited for his legal anecdote to wind down.

While the others around her were chuckling over the eviction that served as the punchline, she edged forwards. "Judge Lowe!" She thought she managed a good facsimile of enthusiastic delight. "What did you think of the Romantics lecture on Thursday evening?"

He blinked at her, momentarily taken aback. "What?"

"The Romantics lecture," she said, trying to mimic Penny Finley's tones. "You seemed most fascinated."

"Romantic lectures? Woman, I have no idea what you're blithering about."

"But you were there," Miss Miller said, widening her eyes and feigning confusion.

"The Phipps affair was Thursday evening," one of the hangers-on murmured.

"I know," the judge snapped at him, before turning back to glare at her. "I assure you that I was in the Grand Chamber until gone ten." He looked over her critically. "I think you might be having a moment.

Understandable, at your age. Now, please excuse me." He turned his back on her.

Miss Miller slunk away in apparent humiliation, letting the judge's sycophants snigger. Once they'd settled back into their oblivious smugness, she faded back from the party, and, as arranged, settled herself in the house's day room with an interesting treatise.

After twenty or so pleasant minutes, Mendez appeared. "I hope that was not too draining, Mary. The Ornithological Society has long been my haven of calm, gentle sanity. My clients are not typically the sort who would ever fit in to such an environment."

"They were a fascinating collection," she said.

Mendez winced. "Ah. Yes. Sorry."

She made an effort to soften her tone a little. "Mr. Koehler was actually rather charming. A very intelligent man. Worth the price of admission. The rest were no more abrasive than any other society crowd, really. These things are sent to test us."

"Speaking of which, did you discern anything?"

"They all have superb alibis. Mr. Wallis was playing the fool in front of a crowd on stage, Mr. McKnight was in a busy restaurant bloviating at an unfortunate conductor, Mrs. Finley was . . . boating, I suppose, with her husband and a captive audience of a score of chefs and waiters, Mr. Koehler was entertaining an octet of German bankers, and Judge Lowe was in chambers in front of several lawyers, a jury, and other court officers. Is there a chance that one of them engaged someone to steal the item for them?"

Mendez sighed. "It's not impossible, but really, there would have been very little time to arrange it. The thief did not need to search anywhere. Only the drawer containing the piece was touched, and that was forced, with a knife by the looks of it. There are more than thirty

drawers in that particular secure cupboard. Nothing else was stolen. My security man didn't hear a thing, so there was no rummaging, no hesitation. That's a very precise theft to arrange in less than sixty minutes. The piece should have been in my safe, but my mind was on the urgency of the call. I suppose we all get a little stupid where family seem to be concerned. This is a blow.
Ah, but it's absolutely not your fault. Honestly. I'm extremely grateful for the efforts you've gone to."

"If we rule out an accomplice... Well. There *is* a way that one of them in particular could have stolen your carving."

Who does Miss Miller suspect, and why?

HINTS:

a) None of the suspects had identical siblings.

b) Each alibi was verifiable by at least half a dozen honest witnesses.

c) The urgent call that diverted Ezekiel Mendez was a distraction, a bureau message runner with a note claiming his sister was at a certain hospital following an accident.

d) George Wallis's character Pantaloon originated in the Commedia dell'arte *masquerades, and is an old merchant with a hook nose and a white goatee.*

e) Demetrius Cabrera frequently had to accept dinner invitations from wealthy patrons and donors, a part of the job he often likened to prostitution.

f) Penelope Finley's husband James always booked out whole restaurants whenever he dined, because he was terrified of vengeful relatives of enemies he'd had killed.

g) Marcellus Koehler steered his Deutsche Bank visitors away strictly from all morally compromising activities, much to their disappointment.

h) Mitchell Lowe was pressing strongly for the death penalty in the Phipps case, a sentence which was well beyond the ordinary for a relatively minor offence.

i) Ezekiel Mendez had no intention of leaving recovery of the stolen netsuke *to police, even if clear evidence had proved available.*

HORTON & CREAK

No. 41

E very comment was a variation on the same theme. "I just don't understand why anyone would want to kill him."

Edwin Coggen had been a popular forty-four-year-old mid-level manager at Horton & Creak, a venerable company that specialized in the regional transport of goods. The firm's owners were quite influential, and were very keen that the police department did right by their slain employee. Accordingly, the last twenty-four hours had provided Inspector Parnacki with an unusually detailed file.

The victim had been found in his office, at his desk, covered in coffee and blood. The time of death was thought to be around six thirty in the evening, when most staff had already gone home. He'd

been killed with a thin garrote which had cut into the flesh at the front of his throat. The weapon had been left in situ, a device improvised from a roll steel wire rather than a professionally made strangler's tool. The wire easily could have been taken from the firm's own stores, but no one could be certain that this was the case.

Coggen's particular area of responsibility had been lumber, an important but intrinsically simple side of the business. The same dozen lumber firms had been on Horton & Creak's books for a decade or more, and their output never varied. His drivers dealt with a parcel of supervisors, who, in turn, worked with his route planners, Alan Gates and James Weedon. Gates and Weedon worked for Coggen directly, but only came to him when problems arose. Most of the man's time had been taken up in meetings with other section managers, preparing reports for his director, and helping the route planners when there was an issue.

Coggen's home life had been just as uneventful. His wife was a year his junior and his children were both in their early twenties, and employed in other departments at Horton & Creak. Fishing had been Coggen's only hobby outside the home. He paid a small annual subscription for one of the spots at the reservoir, and the fishermen on either side of his berth seemed as baffled as everyone else. Apparently Coggen didn't even enter fishing contests.

The man's office reinforced the impression that Inspector Parnacki had received from his reports. It was small and tidy, with the desk up against the far end of the room. The chair that the corpse had been found in was a padded, cloth-covered thing with a swivel base. It had been pushed back against a wall, the pale seat facing toward the door. A child's drawing occupied one small picture frame on the desk, which was spotless, and otherwise held nothing more than a pad of notepaper and a pencil. Shelves above the desk bore an assortment of technical-looking books, and some file folders. There was a large filing cabinet behind the door, accompanied by a hat stand and a small wastepaper bin. At the sides of the room were several chairs, and a large green succulent plant. That was all.

The Inspector made his way over to one of the nearby meeting rooms, where Sergeant Sullivan had placed Alan Gates. The planner was a slight man with mild eyes, although he was obviously in some distress. Parnacki introduced himself to the unhappy fellow, and inquired as to whether he'd noticed anything odd in the conduct of any of his colleagues over the last few weeks.

Gates shook his head. "No, nothing. I've been wracking my brains, trying to think if anything might have happened to give someone a grudge. But everything has been business as usual. Jim and I haven't had any driver issues. The directors have left us alone. There's been nothing. Mr. Wilkins, on paper goods, has had some logistic problems the last day or two that Mr. Coggen was helping with, but if it wasn't him needing something, then it was Mr. Dorey on textiles. It's no secret that lumber is fairly tranquil, and Mr. Coggen was always happy to pick up a bit of slack. He was a good man. Of all the people here, he didn't deserve this."

"Of all the people?"

"You know how it is. We're a big firm, and some people are barely any better than they ought to be. There are blowhards and idlers and miserly lotharios, just as there are anywhere. Mr. Coggen was kind and quietly self-confident, and got on with it, and did his best to make sure we all had what we needed. He treated his family the same way, I understand. I'd be surprised if he'd even killed one of the fish he caught."

"I see. What time did you leave last night?"

"Jim and I leave at five thirty on the dot. We're not eligible for overtime, so Mr. Coggen was always very firm that we not stay an instant late. Wednesdays and Thursdays, we have a beer or two at The Hawthorn over on Broad Street before heading home. We left a little before seven last night."

"And what will happen to his position?"

"It'll be opened to all internal and external applicants. Horton & Creak are happy to promote from within the ranks, and about half the time that's what they end up doing, but they do want to make sure they have the best chap for the job. I won't be applying, anyway. I prefer route work to meetings."

Parnacki thanked the man, and a minute later, James Weedon was in his place. Weedon was a tall, bony fellow with deep-set eyes and a sepulchral voice. He seemed as baffled about recent events as everyone else. "Mr. Coggen was the least offensive man you could ever hope to meet. I don't see any sense in it, but I also don't see anyone just randomly stalking through the building to get to his office in search of a victim. He often stayed a few minutes after time, if he was trying to sort out some issue, but there would have been plenty of people downstairs still, or in other departments. It's very strange, is what it is. Al and I finished work at half five, and we went for our usual midweek drink. I got home about seven thirty. Thursdays is Cribbage Night. Mr. Coggen's job? I might apply. But it's one of the lower-status management roles. I suspect I'd be better served by waiting, and building up my experience further where I am. I'm thinking it over."

After Weedon had gone, the Inspector turned to his notes. There was little mention in his file about the managers that Alan Gates had named, so he set off to find them. Happily, signs on each department's door made the correct locations easy to track down.

Much like the lumber department, the paper goods department was set up as a main room with a personal office set aside for Kevin Wilkins, the manager. It was clearly a larger part of the company, with five clerks and a secretary bustling amongst stacks of filing cabinets and piles of paper. The men were clearly curious about Parnacki, but kept about their business. Wilkins' office door was slightly ajar, so the Inspector knocked and went in.

Wilkins was a handsome man in his late thirties, very neatly groomed, with large blue eyes, fashionable hair and a slightly curled Van Dyke beard. He looked slightly startled for a flickering moment, but a mask of pleasant welcome slipped almost immediately onto his face. "You must be the Inspector," he said, his voice warm and buttery. "Please, do come in." He stood hospitably.

Parnacki shook his offered hand, and entered the room. The office had the same layout as Coggen's, but there was little other resemblance. The shelves behind the desk held a multitude of framed certificates and commendations. The cabinet tops were piled high with orderly stacks of file boxes, and there was a large crate in one corner marked 'samples', filled with reading matter of all forms, from books through to newspapers and advertising circulars. The desk itself was clean and well ordered beneath a somewhat wild covering of papers and stationery tools. Assorted expensive-looking knickknacks were set along the edge, back against the wall. Despite the suggestion of pomp, there was a certain amount of litter—papers balled and tossed on the floor for cleaners to collect, a smoking pipe in a well-filled ashtray, deep coffee stains on various documents and the chair seat, and a tottering heap of files on the floor.

The man noticed Parnacki's glance. "Yes, it's a little chaotic in here at the moment. My deepest apologies. I've been having a little bother with one of my clients, and it's proving tricky to sort out."

"Not at all," the Inspector replied. "I'll only need a couple of minutes of your time. Do you have any idea why someone might have wanted to harm Mr. Coggen?"

Wilkins shook his head. "It's absolutely baffling. Edwin was as straight as an arrow, and agreeable to the point of his own detriment. I can't imagine his death benefiting anyone. To be perfectly selfish for an instant, it's also dashed inconvenient. He'd been helping me untangle the mess I'm in for the last couple of days, and his loss is going to set me back horribly." He sighed. "It's going to be a long night."

"And did you work late last night?"

The man had the grace to look a little embarrassed. "Actually, no. I had an . . . a meeting, across town at four pm, so I left at three. I got home at six. My wife doesn't like me working late, which Edwin was always very understanding about." He brushed a speck of dust off one sleeve, and looked around the room unhappily. "I'm definitely going to miss him."

Robert Dorey was the manager of the textiles department. It was smaller than paper goods, with just three clerks, but it nevertheless had an air of barely suppressed chaos to it. Boxes and cases and folders and loose papers were stashed all over the place, and the men working amongst them looked stressed and unhappy. They collectively glanced up as Parnacki entered, visibly dismissed him as not immediately irrelevant, and continued about their business.

The manager's office was in much the same state, but where the clerks were clearly feeling stressed, Dorey appeared nearly somnolent. He was in his late fifties, with a comfortable paunch and thinning hair. He swung around in his office chair to face the Inspector, and smiled amiably in welcome. When he spoke to answer Parnacki's questions, his voice was deep and soft. "I worked quite closely with Ed Coggen, yes. He was a very helpful sort, and desperately underworked there in lumber. I'll be frank with you, Inspector. Ed shouldered a portion of my load, as I'm sure his lads have told you, and for absolutely no reason other than our mutual boredom. He truly hated being idle, you know. Whereas I rather enjoy it." He sat up a little straighter. "I've been in this chair for twenty-three years. I did try, at first. Truly. It was made clear that this was as far as I would get, however. Then the rheumatism set in, and overnight my body seemed to age from forty to seventy. I have endured here since then, keeping the cloth flowing despite my perpetual exhaustion. A few more years, and I can finally escape. Without Ed propping me up, they're going to be a lot less tranquil than I would have hoped. No, I can't imagine what anyone might have had to gain from offing the poor devil. It's insane. Plenty of idiots disregarded him, but no one disliked him. I was genuinely fond of him. Last night? Like always. I leave at five, religiously. I'm home by five thirty with my slippers and pipe, not really listening to my wife drone on about the petty ups and downs in the lives of our local residents' relatives."

A few minutes later, the Inspector was comparing notes with Sergeant Sullivan, who had been speaking to other staff who'd had dealings with the dead man. "Everyone seems genuinely baffled, Inspector. I don't think anyone I've spoken to is hiding any grudge against the man."

"That's it," Parnacki said suddenly. "I think I know why Coggen is dead."

Why does Parnacki think that Edwin Coggen was killed?

HINTS:

a) None of the men Parnacki had spoken to had any motive to kill Edwin Coggen. Quite the contrary, in fact.

b) Neither Coggen's superiors nor family were in any way involved in his death.

c) Alan Gates was a shy man, and did most of the lumber paperwork in return for James Weedon dealing with most of the supervisors.

d) Robert Dorey lived in constant pain, and was consequently tired the great majority of the time.

e) James Weedon was a keenly ambitious man, but he paired this with a strong sense of propriety.

f) Kevin Wilkins frequently made free with other men's wives, and was consorting with one of his driver's wives on the afternoon of Coggen's death.

g) There was a reasonable amount of criminal activity around the reservoir, but the victim was not involved in it.

h) Edwin Coggen's director, a man named Roderick Horne, had lived in Switzerland for three years during his twenties, working in sales for a clock-making company.

i) The Inspector came to his deduction through his observations.

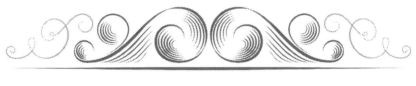

THE BAXTER AFFAIR

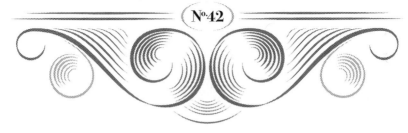

No·42

F elicia Baxter was in her thirties, and she seemed more annoyed than distraught at her recent bereavement. Nevertheless, she was quite determined to get answers to questions that the police, so far, seemed loath to actually ask. "My father could be difficult at times, Mrs. Warren. Like most men. We were cordial, I suppose, rather than close. But if he was no saint, he was no great rogue either. He certainly didn't deserve to be drowned like a dog."

"The police suggested that he had been drinking," Emma said carefully, and took a sip of her water.

"It's a convenient way of explaining off the irregularities. A happy thing for them that the body was in the water four days, so there's no way of being sure. Father greatly disliked being drunk, however. It seems as unlikely as his being in that area of town to begin with. He placed great importance on seemliness, and went to efforts to avoid any potential embarrassment. Why would he be so incapably drunk next to a canal in a warehouse district? It's meaningless."

"Yes, I can see that. Did he have enemies?"

Miss Baxter shrugged. "There were certainly people he'd mightily irritated. His old business partner for one, and my cousin Damian for another. But neither of them seem likely prospects. Karl—Karl Santiago—is over seventy now. He's has had twenty years to get over their failed import business. As for Damian, not only was he written out of Father's will, but he ran off to Paris with a bunch of filched knickknacks two years ago, and hasn't been heard from since."

"What happened with your cousin?"

"He's a degenerate. Hopelessly addicted to

gambling, with sidelines in opium and whores. Father warned him over and over, and eventually had to cut him off. That's when he assembled his little swag bag and fled. Damian's sister, Maria, had been cloistered away in a nunnery for fifteen years by then. It was all horribly predictable. Their father, Roger Dawe, was always a drunkard, but after Aunt Hettie took her own life, he fell to pieces. Damian was thirteen, and Maria just ten. Roger clung on for three more years, and did a lot of damage in that time."

"It sounds horrible."

"Moderately horrible, yes."

Emma jotted a note or two. "So, apart from cousin Damian and Karl Santiago, you can't think of anyone who might have wanted to harm your father?"

"In the past, perhaps. He retired three years ago though, and so far as I know, hasn't made any waves with any of his shareholdings. So there seems no likely vengeful colleague lurking in the wings. My mother holds no particular ill-feeling toward him. Do golfers kill each other over missed putts? It seems unlikely."

"So, let's look at other possible reasons for a murder. Who stands to benefit from his estate?"

Miss Baxter shrugged. "My mother and I get the house and various provisions for security, of course. We'll be perfectly comfortable. Damian would have done well, but as I said, he was written out. Maria is entitled to a decent share, which she's already said she's giving to her abbess. My other aunt, Ina, gets something with her husband, Alex, as do their daughters, Kath and Frieda, but they're quite well off already. Then there's various small bequests to associates, friends, and so on. None of it seems worth killing over."

"We may learn more when the will is read tomorrow," Emma said.

"You can be here for that, yes? Two thirty. It'll give you a chance to meet everyone."

"I'll be here. In the meantime, I'm going to have another look over the area where your father was found."

Despite her best efforts, the hours that Emma spent in Whiteside among the warehouses and canal paths offered no hints. Just row after row of dilapidated storage buildings, some busy with workers, others clearly in disuse. From what she could see, and from occasional comments from garrulous warehousemen, most of the buildings in the area were long-term storage of hardy imperishables—building supplies, pipework, cordwood, and things of that nature. It made sense. Warehouses for expensive, thief-tempting items tended to cluster together for group security, so it stood to reason that low-target goods would end up together as well.

There certainly didn't seem to be any particular reason for Don Baxter to have been there of his own initiative. There weren't even any obvious bars or brothels. On the other hand, a quiet, run-down storage district did make for a sensible place to dump a corpse.

The next day, Emma dressed in unobtrusive dark clothing suitable for a grieving domestic, and settled herself in the room where the lawyer was preparing for the reading. From the far corner she'd picked, she would be able to see people coming in, and still get a decent view of them as the proceedings unfolded. Miss Baxter was waiting by the door, ready to greet arrivals clearly so that Emma could identify them, and her friend, Bridget Radcliffe, was in a nearby chair, offering quiet support.

The first in was her mother, Hester. The woman was in her fifties, tall and elegant in her dark clothing. She greeted her daughter warmly, and exchanged pleasantries with Miss Radcliffe, but there was a strong sense of reserve about her. If she was mourning—or celebrating—

the loss of her husband, she was keeping it well hidden.

Shortly afterwards, Miss Baxter's aunt arrived with her family. The husband, Alexander Hayes, had the look of a banker. Despite being in his fifties, he was still slender and straight-shouldered, and his silver-flecked hair was short and neat. His clothing was suitably reserved, but his shoes were extremely expensive, and his gold-bordered cufflinks looked to be ebony or perhaps obsidian, matching his elegant tiepin. Aunt Ina was a few years younger, and although equally well dressed, there was nothing blatantly expensive about her clothing. Her clutch, however, was trimmed in silk and pearls, all black. Unlike the other arrivals, she actually looked miserable. She sat next to Hester, and pulled her husband down after her.

The Hayes daughters, Kath and Frieda, were a few years younger than Felicia Baxter. They entered arm in arm, chattering away. Although their voices were discreetly quiet, there was no hint of grief about either of them. Kath, the younger, had light brown hair, while her sister was a few shades darker. Their husbands had not joined them, and there was no sign of Frieda's young son.

A pair of older men that Emma knew to be golfing buddies followed a few minutes later, Jack Burks and Ted Bowers. They, too, were expensively dressed, and they bore unhappy expressions. They offered condolences to Felicia and then to her mother, and took seats toward the rear of the room. From what Miss Baxter had said, Burks owned a couple of hotels, while Bowers was a socialite turned family man. They'd been common guests of the Baxter household.

The last arrival was Maria Dawe, in full habit. She was a very thin, nervous-looking woman with pallid skin and dark circles around her eyes. Her only ornamentation was a simple wooden cross on a leather thong around the neck of her habit. She murmured a quiet word or two to Miss Baxter, and sat near the door, clearly uncomfortable in the unaccustomed company.

Once everyone was settled, the family lawyer, a man named Edwards, stood up with a nervous cough. He was a tall, ungainly man with a fringe of white hair around his pate, and melancholy eyes. He hemmed and hawed a bit, looking over the group, and shuffled his papers. Finally, he cleared his throat again. "Ladies and gentlemen, we are gathered here today for the reading of the last will and testament of Mr. Donald Baxter." His eyes settled on the nun. "Sister Maria, would you offer us a blessing?"

The nun nodded. "Of course," she said. She had the soft, husky voice of protracted childhood weeping. She stood, and the rest of the room stood too. "Hail Mary, full of grace, the Lord is with thee. Blessed art thou amongst women. Holy Mary, Mother of God, pray for us sinners, now and at the hour of our death. Amen."

"Amen," the room dutifully repeated, and all sat, eyes returning to Mr. Edwards.

"Thank you," the lawyer mumbled. "Now. Let us proceed." He shuffled some more paper. "'I, Donald Ignatius Baxter, being of sound mind and body, do hereby declare...'"

The reading went on for about twenty minutes, and contained no particular surprises. Miss Baxter and her mother were provided for as expected, and the bulk of the remaining share certificates and bonds were divided between Ina and Alexander Hayes, Kath Thurrard, Frieda Clark, and Maria Dawe. Burks and Bowers got a selection of physical goods, most notably equal shares of Baxter's wine cellar, and some good artworks. As an apparent afterthought, a portrait of the deceased as a young man was left to Karl Santiago, the old business partner.

Although Emma watched everyone carefully throughout the entire process, no one gave any sign of either surprise or dismay at any of the bequests. When Mr. Edwards finally finished, Ted Bowers had tears standing in his eyes, and Ina Hayes was quietly sobbing against her husband's shoulder. The lawyer sat down, and Emma stood up. Everyone turned to look at her.

"Mrs. Warren?" Miss Baxter's voice was curious, but not hostile.

"Please forgive my intrusion at this unhappy time," Emma said. "If I may ask one question, I think I will be able to settle the matter of your father's death."

What is Emma suspicious of?

HINTS:

a) The question Emma wants to ask is not aimed at Miss Baxter.

b) Mr. Edwards had been the Baxter family lawyer for forty years. He was a socially awkward man, and had not been in front of a court in the last decade.

c) Maria Dawe had only left her nunnery twice in the last fifteen years, and found both experiences thoroughly dreadful.

d) Alexander Hayes had never been particularly fond of his wife's family.

e) As a child and young woman, Ina Hayes had frequently hated her conceited older brother, but they had become closer as adults.

f) Don Baxter had never been particularly interested in Kath or Frieda, a sentiment that the nieces had merrily returned.

g) Ted Bowers once shot a servant's foot off, but his father managed to cover the affair up with large amounts of money.

h) Jack Burks used his hotels to provide cover for the distribution of smuggled alcohol brought in from abroad.

i) Bridget Radcliffe had been Felicia Baxter's devoted friend since the pair's school days.

j) Hester Baxter had never felt oppressed by her husband, and likened his loss to the departure of a long-serving staff member.

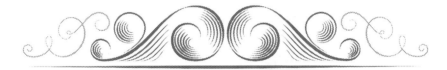

THE MAN IN THE BARREL

Nº·43

'**L**AND DEVELOPER FOUND DEAD IN BARREL', screamed the newspaper headline. 'Paddington Parnacki on the case!'

Inspector Parnacki sighed and tossed the paper into his waste bin. Muttering to himself about drug-addled ne'er-do-wells, he pushed aside a report into a body found in the river ten days ago and looked over the details from the Costello crime scene. Chase Costello, 52, had indeed been found dead in a barrel hidden in a small dockside shack, having gone missing some two weeks previously. According to the reporting officer, the victim had an expression of terror frozen on his face.

The death was due to a single stab wound to the heart, made by a perfectly ordinary kitchen knife, which had been left in the wound.

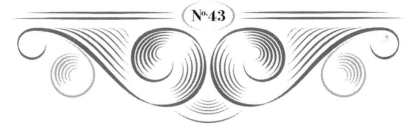

No useful evidence remained on it. There was blood inside the barrel but none around it, and Parnacki felt it safe to assume that the murder had been committed elsewhere.

Costello's wife, son, brother, and business partner were all mentioned in the man's will, but as it transpired, there wasn't much for him to leave. Despite his flamboyant and predatory public image, Costello had been close to financial ruin. Almost anyone who'd had financial dealings with the man or his company could have had good reason to want him dead.

Officers had spoken to all the principals. Dessie Costello, his wife, had returned that very morning from a week-long visit to her parents and siblings in her old home town. Aristos Williams, his business partner, had also been out of town for several days on a last-minute trip to try to keep the business from collapsing. Roman Costello, his brother, had been off hunting. Oscar Costello, his son, divided his time between his job and his lady friend and social life. Olivia Aleman, Oscar's mother, had remarried after splitting up with Chase Costello and was now a housewife who cared for her husband's school-age children from his own former marriage. Luke Aleman, her husband, was a teacher. He was currently abroad with a party of schoolchildren.

Parnacki decided to spend the day talking to everyone in person.

At the victim's large house, the Inspector was greeted by Dessie Costello, the widow. She was dressed in black, and seemed reasonably well composed. According to his notes, she was in her early thirties.

"I want you to find the beast who did this," she told Parnacki. "I loved my husband very much, and this has broken my heart."

Parnacki assured her that he would do everything possible to find the murderer.

"When Chase vanished, I feared the worst. He was never shy about taking the things he wanted, and people get so jealous and spiteful if someone is forthright about being successful. I dare say some of his dealings were a little sharp, but that is the world of business."

"Did your husband mention any threats?"

She shook her head. "Nothing in particular, no. Ari might know more." Her expression softened momentarily, then closed up again. "That's Aristos Williams, Chase's partner," she added quickly. "I don't know him well."

"I see," Parnacki said. "Did you ever hear them talk of such dangers?"

"No. Chase kept business away from home. I only ever met Aristos at functions and the like."

"What about Mr. Costello's family?"

"We weren't close to them. Between you and me, I think they envied him. After the divorce, Oscar was brought up by Olivia, his mother. She tried to turn him against poor Chase. Things became even more difficult for him after we married. Chase's brother, Roman, was just uninterested. They were very different people. I'm afraid that the last couple of weeks have been hard for all of us, though."

Parnacki's next port of call was Olivia Aleman's house. She was in her late forties or early fifties, and lived in a quietly prosperous part of town. Oscar Costello, a shrewd-looking young man, was with her.

"It's a shame that he was killed," Olivia said. "Divorcing me was the best thing Chase ever did, but I'm very sad for Oscar."

"Don't worry," her son said. "It's not that much of a loss."

"Don't talk of your father that way, dear. It's not seemly."

"You didn't see eye to eye," Parnacki said.

Oscar scowled. "He wanted me to be a shark like he was. He always put me down for being too 'weak'. I tried to explain to him again and again that basic human decency and weakness were very different things, but he wouldn't have it. As far as he was concerned, other people were just there to be bulldozed."

Olivia sighed. "There certainly wasn't much gentility to Chase. He was charming when he was younger, though, and his roguery was somewhat exciting. I got rather carried away. I realized my mistake eventually, and escaped."

"He deserved everything he got with that new floozy of his," Oscar said. "They've been married five years, and she's been carrying on behind his back for at least four of them."

"Oscar!"

"It's true. Several times I've gone round there to find Dad away, and heard her shushing a man, or had her come to the door all flushed and guilty."

"I see," said Parnacki. "Do either of you know much about his business partner, a Mr. Williams?"

"Aristos? He's a basically decent man," said Olivia. "I always felt that he helped serve as Chase's counterpoint, keeping him from sliding onto the wrong side of the law. I used to see quite a bit of him in the old days."

"I remember him from when I was young," Oscar said. "He was nice to an annoying child."

Parnacki nodded. "And do you see much of your uncle?"

"Uncle Roman, you mean? No, we have very little contact. He vanished as soon as my parents split up. He's a few years younger than my father, and I always rather got the feeling that he only spoke to my mother and me to keep Dad happy. I've seen him maybe twice in the last ten years."

A little later, Inspector Parnacki pulled into the driveway of Roman Costello's lavish home.

"I'm sorry for your loss," Parnacki said to the man, once they were seated in his ornate reception room. "I understand you're a banker."

"Yes," Roman nodded. "I was never sure what Chase saw in land. It's far more efficient to cut out the intermediary and work with money directly. He wanted me to organize him a loan, you know."

"Were you going to do it?"

"I would have tried, of course. He didn't have much unleveraged collateral, but it could have been possible to sort something out."

Parnacki made a note in his pad. "What can you tell me about Chase's nearest and dearest?"

"There's his wife, Dessie. Chase absolutely adored her. She seems pleasant enough."

"You're not married yourself?"

Roman laughed. "Lord, no. Haven't met the right girl yet. Searching for her is too much fun."

"What about other people close to Chase?"

"Well, he had a rather distant relationship with his son, Oscar.

I hardly know my nephew myself—it became hard after his first wife left—but I know that Chase was worried that the boy would never find the backbone to make anything of himself. And there was his business partner, Williams. Charming chap. Bit of a ne'er-do-well, though, I fear."

"Oh? How so?"

"I have it on good authority that he was carrying on with Dessie behind Chase's back."

Parnacki looked at the man sternly. "You didn't tell him?"

"Heavens! Of course not. Chase was hardly known for his fidelity. None of my business."

"I see. Thank you for your time, Mr. Costello."

Aristos Williams met Inspector Parnacki at the offices he had shared with Chase Costello. The man was in his fifties, and neatly dressed. Of all the people Parnacki had spoken to, he seemed the most genuinely saddened.

"I was fond of Chase," Williams said. "He undoubtedly had a ruthless streak, but he was a loyal friend, and very entertaining company."

"Did he have any enemies?" asked Parnacki.

"Oh, most certainly. Few people did deals with him and came off the better for it. There will also be several competitors celebrating this afternoon, I'm sure."

"Do you think one of them might have killed him?"

"In such a byzantine fashion? No, I doubt it."

"What do you know of his family?"

"He was married twice. His first wife, Olivia, was quite nice, but she was his age, so their marriage didn't last. He had a son with her, Oscar. The boy took after his mother. Pleasant, sensitive lad. Chase remarried a few years ago. Dessie is young, beautiful, and I suspect a little bored. He also has a brother, Roman, who he's quite close to."

"And what of yourself?"

"You mean family? I have a wife, a son who seems determined to become a professional astronomer, and three daughters aged between fourteen and twenty-two." He laughed. "Between home and here, I rarely get a moment to myself. I also have a sister who lives a few hours away with her family. We all get together at holidays, either here or there."

"So how would you characterize your marriage?"

Williams paused for a moment, the smile fading from his face. "You really mean that, don't you? I can't imagine what you've heard, but I adore my wife. I know Chase was a philanderer, but I saw the damage that did first-hand. I'd never inflict that pain on anyone, let alone Maddie."

"Of course," said Parnacki, his voice soothing. "I'm simply trying to get a clear picture."

"All right," said Williams grudgingly.

"What was Chase working on before he vanished?"

"We'd just purchased a large parcel of land near the lake. He intended to build some upmarket homes on it, once he had secured permission."

"I'd like to take a look at that land, if you don't mind," Parnacki said.

"By all means." Williams jotted the address down for him.

When Parnacki found his way to the land, he discovered that it was still lightly forested. The only structure on it was an old wooden cabin. He made straight for it.

Inside, the cabin was surprisingly comfortable. There was a wood-burning stove with an oven and hotplate, a made-up bed, a table with two chairs, and even a wash tub. Several books were on the table, along with two open bottles of beer. One of the chairs was covered with dried blood.

Parnacki permitted himself a short grin. "Gotcha," he said.

Who is the murderer, and how does Parnacki know?

HINTS:

a) The various testimonies are mutually exclusive.

b) Chase's likely time of death is significant.

c) Dessie was having an affair.

d) Oscar and Aristos were fond of each other, and got on well.

e) Chase was not murdered by any of his business enemies.

f) Luke Aleman had nothing to do with the crime.

g) The case Parnacki was working on before this one is related.

THE EYE OF FIRE

Nº·44

The Eye of Fire was a dazzling ruby the size of a baby's fist, currently set in a lavish gold surround. Mayor Williams stood by the piece, basking in its reflected glory as he thanked donors for coming to the party. It was on loan from a major collection somewhere, and Miss Miller shuddered to imagine how many strings the mayor must have pulled to achieve the coup.

Like most attendees, Miss Miller had been brought to the event by the gem. Unlike the others, however, she wasn't interested in gawking, and politics certainly weren't of relevance. Persistent whispers—a friend of a friend of a cousin, and so on—had it that the piece was going to be stolen in a daringly brazen snatch calculated to embarrass the mayor colossally. That was certainly worth putting in an appearance for.

So Miss Miller had come out to the function, obtained a nice pot of tea from an obliging waiter, and positioned herself at a table with a clear view of the stage. The event itself, such as it was, proved singularly dull. A number of deeply self-important people took the stage and spoke about how wonderful they were, before praising the mayor for his wisdom, foresight, tolerance, piety, responsibility, level-headedness, forthrightness, and, quite possibly, his shoe size. Miss Miller did her best not to listen, instead scrutinizing the attendees, and attempting to discern facts about them.

The man in the fine blue pinstripe suit, for example. About 5ft 8in tall, he was doing his best to look like a gentleman of business or even leisure, but his massive shoulders and arms indicated someone

who worked at a physically demanding job. His parade-ground perfect posture surely marked him as having military training. Given his short haircut and cleanness of his lip and chin, it seemed likely that he was still serving. White in his hair put his age around fifty, and his presence at the event suggested that he was an officer— career colonel most likely, given the comparatively low value of his shoes.

The surprisingly tall young woman in aquamarine was another interesting case of misdirection. She must have been 6ft, with a long cascade of loosely curled golden hair that both tumbled down her back and obscured most of her face. That and the high-fashion dress she was wearing ensured she would be the focus of male attention. Her handbag, though, was unusually generous in size, a definite fashion faux pas. She moved with uncommon precision and grace as well, despite her three inches of heel, and her tight outfit revealed an extremely athletic physique. All in all, to Miss Miller she looked like nothing so much as an acrobat pretending to be a silly girl.

Then there was the black-haired waiter, with green eyes like gimlets, and a tell-tale bulge under the left side of his jacket. He gave every appearance of working the crowd along with the others, but never quite seemed to pick up a tray or deliver a drink. Instead, he spent much of his time scanning the room, his face utterly blank. Security, for certain. Was he the mayor's man or was he providing security for some other purpose? The former seemed more likely, but Miss Miller was in no position to find out for certain. At 6ft on the nose, he was no one to be tangling with, and he looked like the type who'd had his sense of fun removed at birth.

There were no maids or cleaners in evidence, but every so often a cook's assistant came to refresh canapés or clear away dirty plates. There were several of them in evidence, all in the same gleaming white jackets and hats. They had a harried look about them, one and all, suggesting a certain strictness on the part of the chef. One in particular, a mousey young woman no taller than 5ft 6in, seemed to be on the brink of tears whenever she entered the room.

Eventually, the guests were seated comfortably and the mayor took to the stage in person. He was greeted with rapturous applause. The champagne had been flowing freely all evening, and the crowd were feeling generous with their bonhomie. Never one to buck a trend, he started with a selection of choice anecdotes to show off his magnificence.

And then the lights went out.

There were gasps and a few shrieks, and the room erupted into chaos. Glass shattered loudly, and several women screamed. Doors slammed. There were more screams, and one howl of pain. "QUIET," bellowed a commanding voice. As the hubbub stilled, the speaker added, "Everybody, stay exactly where you are."

Moments later, the lights flicked back on again—an impressively swift recovery on the part of the mayor's team. More gasps were heard around the room. As people started muttering to each other, the fake waiter stepped on to the stage, brandishing a revolver and a police badge. "Nobody move," he said.

Miss Miller took advantage of the expectant hush to look around. The Eye of Fire, of course, was gone. So was the woman in aquamarine. She wasn't the only one—several people had clearly fled as soon as the lights went out—but she was easily the most notable. The police officer had spotted her absence, too. His face fell and his shoulders slumped, although he didn't say anything aloud.

It seemed like an awfully long way for someone to get from the stage to the door in the brief time between the glass breaking and the lights going back up, however. Even for an acrobat. Miss Miller looked toward the stage thoughtfully. Slipping into an empty seat in the pitch black would have been a very risky move. If nothing else, those around you would notice. Hmm. Only a reasonably small selection of people were actually standing, though. The mayor and his assistant were on the stage, looking utterly horrified. The mayor could probably feel his career crumbling around him already.

The policeman was the other person with them, and he appeared resigned, verging on defeated.

There were a few others in the room who were not in their seats. Foremost among them was the probable colonel, who was just a few feet from the front of the stage. He was peering around the room with a look of furious concentration, as if determination alone could mystically reveal the stolen ruby. Fortunately, he was also helping to keep the room in order. If anyone so much as shifted uncomfortably in their chair, he fixed them to the spot with a terrifying glare. When he tried the trick on her, she smiled at him sweetly. He immediately paled slightly, and turned his gaze elsewhere.

A slim woman in a dark dress was also standing up. Her position rather implied that she had been talking to someone at a table nearby, but no one around her was paying her any particular attention. At 5ft 8in she was slightly taller than the average for a woman, but in most ways she seemed rather insignificant—hair of medium length and undistinguished shade, clothes of decent but not showy quality, a pleasant face that would be unlikely ever to drive men to obsession, and shoes with barely any heel. Everything about her suggested a safe, comfortable personality.

A pair of men were also standing up, near the small service bar. Despite their proximity, they gave no appearance of familiarity with each other. One, somewhere in his twenties, had clearly been a little too free with the mayor's champagne. He had loosened his tie and unbuttoned his jacket, and stood there swaying gently, all 5ft 10in of him, occasionally blinking. His signet ring suggested a college education, and the cut of his clothing marked him as being from a wealthy, established family. There was a hint of dissolution in the length and shape of his hair, but his fingers, rubbing his elbow, appeared nimble.

The other man looked older and considerably less free-spirited. His soul appeared to be as tightly buttoned as his shirt. He was a couple of inches shorter than his accidental companion, and the rigidity of his posture suggested powerful disapproval. A slender man with hollow cheeks, thin lips, and over-large eyes, he gave the strong impression of being a priest of one sort or another. His nostrils flared every time he inhaled. His dress was as sober as his attitude seemed to call for, punctiliously correct in every matter of decorum without permitting any deviation for individuality or ornamentation. If he was indeed a preacher, the party would have given him plenty of material for a series of fiery pulpit sermons. But why was he standing by the drinks?

A skinny young cook's assistant was standing against the wall on the other side of the room from the pair of men. He was wearing the same outfit as the other assistants, and the same look of worry. From what Miss Miller could see of his shoes, they looked like flat, brown affairs. Clearly, being tardy in returning to the kitchen was a

serious fault in the chef's eyes. The lock of black hair escaping from the hat would probably not help his cause any, either. It was difficult to be sure, of course, but he looked to be about an inch taller than the possible priest. She tried to give him a reassuring smile, but he plainly had no intention of looking up from the floor, which nevertheless refused to swallow him whole.

Nearest of all to the door was a young woman in a maid's apron. She was clutching a dustpan and brush and darting uneasy glances here and there. Her brown hair was pulled back tightly from her face and fastened in a low bun. She had intelligent pale eyes that, at the moment, were full of concern. Her height, at 5ft 7in, was not exceptional, but her cheekbones suggested that she would mature into a woman of some beauty. Miss Miller clucked to herself. Life was not always easy for a pretty maid, not always easy at all. But that was hardly the matter at hand.

Miss Miller glanced around the room again, and came to a decision. She stood up and, ignoring the colonel's protestations, walked swiftly to the front of the stage. The policeman looked to the mayor, who nodded, hope flickering briefly across his face. "What is it, Ma'am?" the policeman asked.

"Well," said Miss Miller quietly, "I'm almost completely sure that the thief is still in this room. I can tell you who you should investigate first, too."

Who does Miss Miller suspect, and why?

HINTS:

a) The thief is a master of disguise.

b) The thief had arranged for the lights to go out.

c) The lights came back on far more quickly than the thief had anticipated.

d) The colonel is not party to the robbery.

e) The thief was the woman in turquoise.

f) As well as preparing the lights, the thief also concealed some useful disguise material in the room.

g) The thief is still in the room.

THE GRAND HOTEL

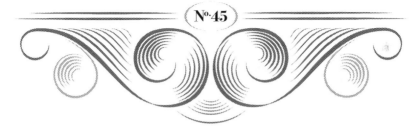

There was something uniquely unpleasant about luxury hotels, Inspector Parnacki thought. A certain bland, over-opulent sameness that tended to leave one feeling somehow outside of reality. Certainly some of the nastiest crimes seemed to take place in such settings. Did the bubble of insulation lead people in this environment to suppose that they were safer from consequence and reprisal? Or was it that long exposure to such languid excess fooled them into thinking that they were somehow lordly? He sighed to himself. It seemed more likely to assume that those who could afford to spend time in such places were somewhat dehumanized compared to the population at large.

Either way, the Grand was a fairly typical example of the species. Thick carpets and lavishly gilded and chromed features were all set off by paintings, statuary, flowers, and frescos. A number of clearly

self-impressed guests milled around the lobby, trailing furs and flunkies. Bellhops and busboys darted everywhere, dressed in the staff uniform—a white shirt, shoes and gloves, with a sky-blue jacket and tie, cummerbund, trousers, and a round, brimless drummer-boy cap.

Braden Smallwood had made his money in transport. Having inherited his father's fortunes and businesses at a comparatively young age, he had turned his attention to rail and shipping. He quickly became one of the wealthy elite of the region through a winning combination of high prices, poor service, and shoddy treatment of his staff. If more workers died in his service than did working for the next four largest of his competitors combined, that apparently was a perfectly comfortable burden to be borne.

He had accrued plenty of aggrieved enemies, but money purchased a lot of protection from the poor, and a lot of forgiveness from the rich. Occasionally some hapless enraged parent, spouse, sibling or child would get close enough to hurl mud or insults, but neither had ever ruffled Smallwood's feathers. Inevitably, the only result would be a lengthy jail sentence for the offender.

Now it seemed as if someone had finally caught up with the man and had spent some time expressing their displeasure with unusual severity. Parnacki made his way through the lobby, shooing off the over-eager bellhops, and proceeded to the second floor.

Smallwood was in Room 16, its doorway flanked by officers. It proved to be a large suite in style with the rest of the hotel. A very large four-poster bed dominated one room, while the second was given over to an ornate yet comfortable reception area, which included two wingback armchairs set near the lively fireplace, a loveseat, and an attractive divan against one wall. Large windows gave the suite a light, airy feel.

The corpse was in one of the armchairs, naked above the waist. A pair of scissors jutted from one eye socket, but from the mess that had been made of the chest area, they had clearly been used to stab him repeatedly as well. Smallwood's suitcases had been hurriedly searched, the contents scattered around the room. At least one shirt had ended up in the fireplace, going by the remnants of burnt white cuff at the edges of the grate. It was fortunate that a larger fire hadn't started.

Parnacki paced around the suite thoughtfully while he waited for his first interviewee. Apart from the scattered contents of the suitcases and the blood around and beneath the corpse, nothing else appeared to be out of order anywhere. There were no personal items in the bedroom or bathroom, suggesting that Smallwood had only recently arrived. In the reception room, a pot of coffee, a tray of sandwiches and

a bowl of fruit jostled for table space with a large bottle of champagne and a pair of glasses.

A knock at the door indicated the arrival of Alison Farris, a wide-eyed maid in her early twenties. Parnacki escorted her to the suite opposite, which the hotel had enthusiastically set aside for his use. Like that of the staff downstairs, her outfit was blue and white, although it looked slightly untidy, and had a large white pinafore over the top of it all.

"I understand you attended to Mr. Smallwood earlier this afternoon," Parnacki said to her, once the introductions were out of the way.

"Yes, sir," Alison said. She was clearly nervous.

"Maybe you could talk me through that." Parnacki smiled kindly.

"Of course, sir."

Parnacki nodded encouragingly.

"Oh! Well, I was told by Lucille that sixteen had a problem with the pillows, and to get myself up here and see what was wrong—oh, Lucille, she's the floor manager for the afternoon shift, and she's got quite the stern reputation, and well deserved too, so of course I didn't want to do anything what might annoy her, so I came straight over,

as you would. So I knocked on the door of sixteen, and he told me
to come in, all impatiently, so that's what I did, but not impatiently,
obviously, that would be rude and we can't have that, it's really
important to make the guests feel at home." She drew in a very deep
breath. "So I came into the room, and the guest was there, standing
in the doorway between the reception and the bedroom, holding one
of the pillows, not like he was cuddling it or anything, but more like
it smelled or something, because it was out at arm's length, and he
had this offended look on his face. I could see that he hadn't touched
his coffee or his sandwiches that he'd made such a fuss over, and sure
enough, 'This is filthy', he tells me, and my first thought is to assure
him that it most certainly isn't because I put it there myself not two
hours ago and I'd never put a dirty pillow out for a guest, but I know
I'm never supposed to be arguing with a customer, so of course I just
apologize, and tell him I'll replace it immediately, and I'm very sorry,
and I can't imagine how it might have got there." Another shuddering
breath. "I left the room immediately with the pillow, and of course
it was every bit as spotless as I'd thought, but there's no telling with
some people, so I went back to the linen room and found a spare
pillow and a clean cover, and I put them together, and then I took the
replacement back to sixteen, knocking on the door and slipping in.
He took it from me, and snorted, then said 'That will do, I suppose', as
though I was getting him to sleep on a chunk of sacking or something,
so I went back, made the bed up, and got out of there, and that's
everything that happened, sir."

Parnacki blinked as she crashed to a halt. "I . . . see. And how did
Mr. Smallwood seem to you?"

"Much like most of the guests, sir. That he'd as soon flay me as kiss
me, if you know what I mean."

"I do indeed. What about the suite, did anything seem out of place?"

"Well, now you mention it, I've never liked that marble bust in sixteen, that one of the explorer, there's something just not right about that man's face, it . . . but I suppose that's not what you mean, sir. No. Everything looked fine inside and out, all spick and span. Apart from the bust. But he always looks like that. So it was all fine."

"Thank you, Miss Farris," Parnacki said. "I'll call for you if I have any more questions."

The maid bobbed her head, and rose to leave. "May I say what a pleasure it was meeting you, Inspector, a pleasure indeed. You're a real gentleman, sir. Good afternoon."

Once he was sure that she was gone, Parnacki permitted himself a rueful shake of the head. Sharper than she seemed, Miss Farris was. Many were.

The next interviewee on his list was Damian Edwards, one of the busboys. Edwards was a rigid-looking man in his early thirties, clean-shaven with black hair and a matching black tie. His carriage was rigorously correct, but he tended to fiddle with the hem of his uniform when he was thinking.

"I understand that you discovered the body, Mr. Edwards," Parnacki said.

Edwards jolted slightly. "I did," he said, his voice soft. "It was..."

Parnacki waited patiently.

"Horrible," the man blurted at last. "Obscene. Disgusting. Sorry. This isn't easy."

Nodding, Parnacki said, "And were you making a delivery to the room?"

"No, actually I was refreshing the fruit bowl in eighteen. I heard what sounded like a violent scuffle coming from next door, so I came to investigate. As I approached sixteen, the handle jerked, and the door was wrenched inward. A man raced out and down the hall away from me. I didn't get a good look at his face, but he was wearing a pinstripe suit, and his hands were bloody. I just stopped dead in the middle of the hall and stared. It simply didn't make sense, and I suppose I froze.

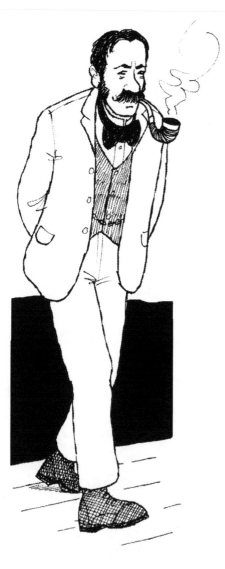

When I came back to myself, I went to investigate in the room, and that's when I found Mr. Smallwood, all chopped up."

"Can you describe the suspect for me?"

"About five foot ten, and quite muscular, with a short beard and moustache. A pinstripe suit, like I said. Dark brown hair."

"Is there anything else that might help us identify him?"

"Not that I saw, I'm afraid."

"And just to double-check, you didn't disturb anything inside the room, did you?"

"No, of course not. I might have steadied myself against the wall when I saw the body, but I certainly didn't move anything."

"Thank you, Mr. Edwards," Parnacki said. "I'll send for you if I have further questions."

Once he was gone, one of the officers outside Room 16 poked his head into 18, where Parnacki was puffing pensively on his pipe. "Are you ready for the shift supervisor, sir? Lucille Clark?"

"No thank you, Officer Mayhew. I don't think we need to bother her just at this moment. I know who and where the killer is."

Who is the murderer, and how does Parnacki know?

HINTS:

a) Parnacki was told several lies.

b) Consider the movements of the suspects.

c) Miss Farris is a little older than she looks.

d) The murderer had a very personal grudge against Braden Smallwood.

e) Smallwood was not robbed of any valuables.

f) This was not the first murder to occur at the Grand.

g) Several items of clothing were tossed into the fire.

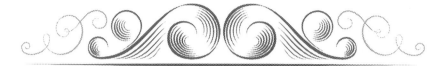

THE TWIN

The robbery at Garland's Fine Jewels was front-page news. A team of men burst in on the very stroke of six in the evening. The manager, Davis Bilton, was closing the shop after the day's work. They were all waving shotguns around and shouting. Bilton was on his own, and capitulated almost immediately with only a bruise for his trouble. The thieves forced him to open up all the locked cabinets, and emptied everything. The heist took less than five minutes. A knot of bypassers watched them run off, but no one dared chase after them. Police arrived on the scene a short while later, with the press hot on their heels.

The men had worn stockings over their heads, but with so many fresh witnesses in place, good descriptions of the robbers were soon circulating around both the police department and the news. The police made the pragmatic decision to cooperate with the press on the case, and provided extra details to help keep the story in the public eye.

Fortunately for his own sanity, Inspector Parnacki was not expected to take statements from the endless flood of concerned individuals who turned up at stations across the city absolutely certain that they knew one or more of the criminals. That information was collated and cross-referenced, then filtered for plausibility before summary reports were passed to his sergeant. Sullivan then went over them a second time, digging into files to narrow down the list of possibilities.

The Inspector was looking over the manager's transcripts of what the robbers had said exactly—there were some curious turns of phrase—when Sergeant Sullivan knocked on the doorframe, a file under one arm.

"Yes, John?"

"Looks like we've got a match for the ringleader of the Garland lads, sir."

"Already? Excellent work, sergeant."

"Thank you, sir. One of our more

reliable sources fingered him as Jeff Sparks. That fits with a number of public suggestions, and he's certainly got the jacket."

"What do we know about Mr. Sparks?"

"He and his brother run a small firm up north, in Sotton. They're careful and they're well represented, so they've been called in a lot, but nothing sticks, not even to their lads. They're very canny about walking the line—no serious injury, no abuse, no over-sympathetic targets. Just businesses, ones that should be insured, with goods that can be moved easily. So they've never quite become enough of a priority to really nail down. They're busy, though. A dozen hits in the last year, with a cluster last December."

"Interesting. Bring Sparks in on suspicion, and let's put him in a line-up. Perhaps Mr. Bilton can confirm his identity."

"Right you are, sir."

The next day, Inspector Parnacki met Davis Bilton in his office. The manager of Garland's was a thirty-four-year-old man of medium height and build, with a slightly pinched face and a heavy bruise on his cheek. He looked nervous, but clearly determined to do his part.

"Thank you for coming in, Mr. Bilton," Parnacki said. "I want to make it absolutely clear to you that you will not be seen or heard by the men I'm going to ask you to look at. They will know that they are being watched, but that is all. You are in no danger. After the entire process has been completed, I will ask you if you see the man who accosted you amongst the suspects. Your identification will be confirmatory rather than accusatory—that is, if you happen to pick someone innocent by mistake, nothing untoward will happen to that man. Do you have any questions?"

Bilton thought for a moment. "I only saw him wearing a stocking. Is that a problem?"

"No, we have arranged for you to see the men both with and without a stocking mask. In your statement, you said that your assailant said, and I quote, 'You mind to keep yourself all nice, my lad, and you'll not be hurt.' Is that correct?"

"That's right, Inspector."

"Excellent. Are you ready?"

The manager nodded and swallowed. "Yes, sir."

"Let's get it done, then."

Parnacki gathered up Sullivan, and the pair of them shepherded the man to the dimly lit viewing room. Sparks was there amongst five other men of similar build and general appearance—strong but not stocky, a little over six feet tall, with a blandly pleasant face, and short brown hair. Several of the men, Sparks included, bore small smiles. They all made plausible robbers, although Parnacki knew that two of them were bank clerks, and one was a florist. A police constable was in there with them, and when the Inspector knocked on the mirrored window, he snapped to attention.

"Please face the light in front of you and take two steps forward," the constable said. The men obeyed. The policeman proceeded to have them, one at a time, turn first to one side and then the other, then to pull on a stocking mask and face all three directions again. Finally, he had each of the six men speak the line that Bilton had confirmed.

The men in the line-up stepped back. "Do you see your attacker?" Parnacki asked, quietly.

Bilton nodded. "Number five," he said, equally quietly.

Number five was Jeff Sparks. "Are you certain?"

"Absolutely positive, beyond any doubt. That's him. That's the man who robbed me."

After Bilton had provided a signed attestation as to his identification and been ushered out of the station, Parnacki asked Sullivan to prepare the suspect for interview.

"Of course, sir," the sergeant said. "He's got his lawyer with him, a smooth fellow named Eagleton, and he's got an alibi."

Parnacki nodded. "Don't they always?"

"I'm trying to confirm it at the moment, sir. Waiting for a call back.

But, well, he says he was at the Elwood Rooms with some friends and family, and a bunch of the great and good saw him there. I'll let you know if it pans out, though."

The Elwood Rooms were extremely expensive, and frequented by the top layers of the city's society. "I see. Thank you, sergeant."

When the Inspector entered the interview room a few minutes later, he found Sparks and his lawyer sitting there looking perfectly at ease. The lawyer leapt to his feet, and shook Parnacki's hand. "The famous Paddington Parnacki! It's a pleasure to meet you at last, Inspector. A true pleasure. Martin Eagleton, of Eagleton and Embling. I'm sure you're as keen to release my client from this unfortunate misunderstanding as he is to get home to his family."

Sparks watched on, his expression of patient benevolence.

Parnacki inclined his head non-committally, and smiled a thin smile. "Good morning, gentlemen. I appreciate your cooperation. I just have a few questions."

"I'm quite sure we've already answered any question you might have," Mr. Eagleton said pleasantly.

"Even so."

The lawyer nodded. "Very well. We can spare the police a little more time. I'd like it recorded that we are doing everything possible to assist you in this matter."

"Of course," Parnacki said, and jotted down a note to that effect. "Now, Mr. Sparks, would you tell me please where you were at 6 pm last night?"

"Come, Inspector. At 6 pm, my client was in the middle of his main course at the Elwood Rooms, as you already know."

Parnacki nodded. The Elwood Rooms was a solid eight miles from Garland's, and the journey would have taken fifteen minutes each way at the very minimum.

Sparks leaned over and whispered something to the lawyer.

Eagleton nodded. "My client would like me to point out that as the restaurant clock turned exactly six, he was having his wine glass filled with a rather palatable '75 Bordeaux by his waiter of choice there, a young Florentine man named Gianni. I am afraid that my client does not recall the man's surname."

Another quick, whispered conference.

"Also, going by my client's own watch, the clock in the restaurant runs precisely ninety-three seconds fast."

Parnacki recorded everything calmly, and turned to the list of people that Sparks had been dining with. "And may I confirm who was at the table with your client at that time?"

"At six precisely?" the lawyer asked.

"Indeed."

Eagleton calmly listed off a dozen names.

Parnacki nodded as he ticked them off the list. One was missing. "The guest list you gave us earlier included Mr. Sparks's brother, Jerrod. Was he absent?"

The lawyer almost managed to suppress a wince. "He was away from the table right then."

"I see. And if I may ask, might it be possible to mistake one brother for the other, say across a dining room, or if his features were somewhat obscured?"

"Well, yes. They are, in fact, identical. Monozygotic. But my client—"

Parnacki permitted himself a moment of satisfaction. "If I may, can your client vouch for his brother's location at the time in question?"

"Naturally. Mr. Jerrod Sparks was making use of the facilities. I am told that he has had a little stomach upset this week."

"I see," Parnacki said crisply. "And precisely how long was your client's brother away from the dining table?"

"Precisely?"

"As precisely as possible."

A slow, evil smile spread across the lawyer's face. "One minute and twenty-three seconds."

Parnacki blinked.

Sparks leaned over to whisper to his lawyer again.

"My client would like me to point out that he was timing his brother's absence, as part of an ongoing joke between the brothers."

"Timing it."

"Indeed, Inspector. And then he announced this duration loudly as his brother returned, to tease him. I'm confident that most of the people who were in the restaurant will recall the incident. After all, how often does one notice identical twins?"

"Quite," Parnacki said shortly. "Would you excuse me a moment?"

"Of course, Inspector. We're happy to help however we can."

Outside the interview room, Sullivan was standing there with a worried expression. He passed the Inspector a sheet of paper that, on closer examination, listed several names confirming Sparks's alibi, including one Gianni Buonarotti, as well as two socialite ladies of impeccable reputation, and one of the mayor's aides. Parnacki took the list back into his office, closing the door behind him, and sat down.

About half an hour later, he leapt up, flung the door open, and called for Sergeant Sullivan. "Are Sparks and his lawyer still there, John?"

"Yes, sir. They seem quite content."

"Excellent. I'm sure of the game Sparks and that lawyer are up to. He's guilty, all right, and that alibi is worthless."

How does Inspector Parnacki think he's broken the man's alibi?

HINTS:

a) Mr. Bilton correctly identified Jeff Sparks as the leader of the group who robbed Garland's.

b) Martin Eagleton was careful to avoid lying to the Inspector. Everything he said was, in fact, true.

c) Gianni correctly informed Sergeant Sullivan that he was serving Mr. Sparks at 6 pm.

d) Jerrod Sparks was on the premises of the Elwood Rooms constantly from 5.15 pm through to 7 pm.

e) Neither Jerrod nor Jeff Sparks possessed any supernatural or similarly unusual abilities.

f) The Garland's robbery was the biggest haul the Sparks crew had landed in five years.

g) The heist was very carefully prepared.

h) No form of aircraft or other outlandish transport was involved.

MATILDA'S
BIRTHDAY

Nº·47

It was a lovely day, sunny with a smattering of harmlessly puffy little clouds, not too hot, and with a pleasant edge of breeze. Perfect for a garden party. Matilda Vincent had been throwing determinedly lavish birthday parties since the age of five, and as her eldest cousin, Miss Miller had been in dutiful attendance all the way through. This year was the thirty-first of them, and the usual suspects were all present, of course. Many of them were good company in small groups, but large gatherings tended to produce bland conversation from all but the most determinedly iconoclastic.

Matilda was currently off with a gaggle of her school chums, all of them giggling away and waving drinks around. Looking over the rest of the crowd, Miss Miller spotted cousin Amelia dutifully smiling as her husband Marlon attempted to charm an unpleasant judge and his extended family. Poor Amelia made constant sacrifices for Marlon's

political career. Not far from the
drinks table, George Wallis was
holding forth in the middle of a
group of hangers-on. He looked
to have lost quite a bit of weight
recently, but he had a bright smile
plastered across his face.

At the entrance to the marble
garden, Olly and Caroline James
were in conversation with the artist
Tracey Kenyon and her new acolyte, a very earnest young man with
unreasonably lovely eyes. Past them, the colonnade of statues ran
toward the edge of the gardens proper, where the copse began. It looked
quietly inviting there off in the distance, and Miss Miller's resolve
wavered until what looked like a small cluster of the party's white
balloons floated away over the trees. Duly reminded of her duty, she
stifled a sigh. Miss Kenyon and the Jameses would be decent company.

Before she could take a step, the people rippled apart and her
friend Oswald Ware appeared in front of her. Fifty-something and of
medium height, he looked particularly dapper today. Even his hair was
slicked back out of the way. Despite this concession, he was clutching
his birding journal, and looked utterly unrepentant about it. "My
dearest Mary," he said, his voice full of relief. "What a delight. How is
the day treating you?"

Miss Miller smiled at him. "Pleasantly enough, Oswald. All the
better for your arrival. Do I take it that you've been scoping out the
ornithological possibilities of Cousin Matilda's grounds?"

"A little, I admit. Nothing of any particular note to report so far,
however. Doves and songbirds, and a glimpse of a distant chicken-

hawk. But how's poor Aubrey doing?"

"Oh, he's feeling very sorry for himself, but he'll be fine. He's loving the minced chicken liver, but rather hating the steam baths. He's already breathing more easily, though, and he'll be clawing up the ottoman again in no time. He's only seven, so the vet was never worried."

A small cough at her elbow prompted her to turn round. Matilda's husband Bobby was starting to thin out on top, but he still looked a lot like the anxious seventeen-year-old she'd met over scones twenty-three years before. "Ah, Miss Miller—"

"There's no need to be formal, Bobby, dear. This is Oswald Ware, an old friend, and he's every bit as odd as I am."

Oswald beamed at that, and held a hand out. "What a compliment! My pleasure to meet you."

"And Oswald, this is Robert Vincent, my cousin by marriage," she said, as they shook hands.

Bobby managed a smile, but his eyes stayed tense. "Any friend of Mary's. Ah, Mary, I'm afraid I need your assistance."

She shot Oswald an apologetic glance. "Of course. You might like to try the woods past the marble garden to the south, Oswald. There's a lovely tribe of cardinals that I've spotted in there a few times."

"Duty calls, eh? Understand completely, my dear. The perils of notoriety! Robert, it was lovely, and don't worry, I'm sure Mary will be able to help." He wandered off, humming to himself.

"I'm sorry about that," Bobby said. "I wouldn't bother you, but..."

"It's perfectly alright, my dear. What's happened?"

He took a deep breath. "Mattie's birthday present has been stolen. A diamond choker."

"I see. It will have been waiting in the salon for the presentation, I assume. Do you know how recently?"

"No more than fifteen minutes. And yes, it was in the salon. The police can be here in an hour or so, they claim, but that could be far too long."

"Let's go and have a look, shall we?"

They made their way round the edge of the party and up the terrace. The salon was above the ballroom, and had a large balcony that looked out over the garden, and the party beneath. When the weather was good, Matilda received her husband's gift on the balcony toward the end of the afternoon, to mark the festivities moving inside to the ballroom. The design scheme this year was white with accents of gold and pink, and if the garden had seemed liberally clustered with streamers and helium-filled balloons, the ballroom was actively festooned. Tables were set out for the high tea to come, and each had to have its own little knot of decorations as well. To Mary's eye, the whole room looked disagreeably like an exploded wedding cake.

The salon was at least more restrained, but it was like stepping into a realm bleached of life. The floor had always been of the palest marble, but the walls had been painted to match, and the grand piano had been freshly lacquered with a brilliant white gloss. Its cover was down, presumably to hide the black keys. Spotless pale cream couches occupied two walls and met at the corner, where a snowy white coffee table held a white wicker basket filled with matching roses and carnations. Several more of the balloons were tied to one end of the basket, also white. A pair of rather fine marble statues, Romanesque ladies in flowing gowns, stood at either end of the couches, looking toward the coffee table. The doors to the balcony were open, the view obscured by white lace drapes.

Miss Miller turned to Bobby, half-expecting him to have become a bleached ghost. "It's a bit stark in here, don't you think?"

He nodded. "The box containing Mattie's choker was wrapped in gold paper and sealed with pink ribbon. The idea was that it would be the absolute focus. It *is* a little overpowering without it."

"Mm. And where was the box?"

He pointed to the flowers, which did have a long indentation down their middle. "In there."

Miss Miller moved up to the table, and had a closer look. The box looked to have been about nine inches long, and a little under three inches wide. There was no hint of gold or pink amongst the flowers. Up close, she could see that even their stems had been painted white. "You've had someone look under and behind everything?"

"Yes, we've been through the place with a very delicate fine comb, and the balcony, too. I've checked in the piano, both keys and mechanism, under and inside the plant pots outside, behind the couches, in every cushion. There's nothing."

"What about off the balcony?"

"There's nothing hanging, and it's directly above the drinks table.

Lloyd would have noticed if a box fell on him."

"Tricky. Has there been anyone acting suspiciously?"

"Not exactly. Theresa saw a woman whose description I didn't recognize coming out of the salon a few minutes before we realized anything was wrong, but she wasn't carrying anything. I sent Iver to see if the woman is still here, and to keep an eye on her."

Miss Miller riffled through her memory for a moment. "Theresa is the girl over there, hovering near the top of the stairs, is that right? A chambermaid?"

Bobby nodded. "That's right."

They left the room, and made their way over to the maid. Oddly enough, she appeared to cheer up as they approached, and dropped a quick curtsey.

"Theresa, this is my cousin Mary. She's helping with the incident. Maybe you could tell her about the woman."

"Sir, ma'am," Theresa said. She had a light, pleasant voice, and a mass of brown curls that kept trying to escape. "I won't pretend to know everyone who visits, but I do recognize some, and I'm absolutely certain I've never seen this lady before. She's maybe as much as thirty, and very beautiful, with the most striking green eyes, and long black hair that swooshes down to near her waist. Her dress matches her hair, and it's ever so slim and elegant. I saw her coming out of the salon, and she noticed me and smiled this huge, happy smile, then turned off down the west wing. The way she walked was like she was almost swaying or some such. She... I suppose you'd say she demanded attention. There was nothing stealthy or sneaking about her. She didn't have the box. It's impossible. There isn't anywhere on her to hide a thing, and her purse is far too small."

Mary felt her eyebrows arching. "Interesting. Do you know if she's still here?"

"Oh yes, ma'am. Mr. Iver waved to me from the door of the small library not five minutes ago. She's in there, and him with her."

"Thank you Theresa, that's a great help," Miss Miller said. "Bobby, let's go and introduce ourselves to this mysterious lady."

They made their way down the hall to the library. Iver was towering just inside the door, as thin and grave as ever. As they entered, he nodded toward the far corner. A few steps further, and the woman came into view. If anything, Theresa had slightly undersold her. She was almost six feet tall in her heels and as slender as a willow, with a cascade of glossy black hair and a sweetly lovely face. Her dress was a sheer, figure-hugging wrap that covered her from throat to ankle and seemed to flow as she moved. It had to have cost a fortune. A string of black pearls hung around her neck, visible mainly by the way they glistened, and she carried a tiny clutch in one hand that barely looked big enough for a pack of cigarettes.

She noticed them, and turned to face them, smiling with apparent delight. The girl had been right, there was absolutely no way she was hiding a long box on her person. "Hello there. Isn't this a wonderful house!" Her voice was slightly smoky, and there was the faintest hint of an accent of some sort.

"Thank you," Bobby managed. "I'm glad you like it. Robert Vincent, at your service."

The woman held her hand out for him to take. "Jeanne Harper. You throw a delightful party, Mr. Vincent."

"My wife deserves the thanks, not me. You must know her from..." He let the question trail off.

"I'm a friend of Caroline's, actually. She couldn't make it, but she assured me you'd be delighted if I came in her stead." Her smile dimpled a little.

"Oh, yes, Caroline James," Miss Miller said.

"Actually, no. Caroline Anstey. I'm so sorry, I didn't get your name."

Mary smiled pleasantly. Caroline Anstey was a vaguely familiar name. A social figure in the city of Bettfield, perhaps? "How dreadfully rude of me. I'm so sorry, my dear. Miss Mary Miller." For just an instant, Jeanne Harper's perfect smile flickered. "And how is Mrs. Anstey?"

"Boating, actually," the woman said. "A sudden and inescapable engagement. She's in great and happy health, though."

"That's good to hear," Bobby said. His voice was a little strangled. "I wonder, Miss Harper, since Caroline has left you high and dry, would you permit me to introduce you around? There are some delightful people here today who would simply love to meet you."

Jeanne Harper playfully pushed Bobby's shoulder. "You darling man. I'm quite content just poking around, though." She paused, and her smile took on a mischievous edge. "I suppose I should level with you. Arabella Coombs has a party coming up soon, and I'm here to spy on your wife's festivities on her behalf. Everyone up and down the coast knows that Tilly's birthday is *the* bash, and Bella is keen not to be too far behind." She flicked a winsome glance at Bobby. "I hope you can forgive me."

Mary nodded thoughtfully. Arabella Coombs was the undisputed queen of Bettfield society, and was in equal parts worshipped and feared in half a dozen cities. A formidable name to throw around.

Bobby coughed awkwardly, his cheeks pink. "Not at all. It's our privilege. Please, poke around to your heart's content."

She dazzled at him. "You really are as lovely as I've heard." She paused for a slow heartbeat. "Perhaps you'd care to give me a little tour?"

"Alas," Mary said quickly. "I need him to fix something for me in the ballroom. Iver over there will be delighted to show you around. Please excuse us."

"Of course," the woman said, and smirked just a little.

Miss Miller took Bobby's arm, and steered him out of the library and toward the stairs down to the ballroom.

As they descended, Bobby cleared his throat. "Well, she seems nice enough, and I suppose Mattie does know some of the Bettfield set."

Miss Miller patted him on the arm. "You're far too trusting, my dear. She's the thief for certain."

"There's no way she has the box. It just not possible. Not in . . . uh, that is, she just doesn't have anywhere to hide it."

"She doesn't need the box."

"But where is it, then? She definitely left the salon without it, and it's not in there, and it's not in the punch."

"Go back to our delightful Miss Harper, Bobby. Tell her you've escaped my disapproving gaze, and be dazzled by her until the police arrive. Consider this a free pass to keep admiring her charms. Just stop her from leaving. I have a good idea of where that box is."

Where does Mary think that the box has been hidden?

HINTS:

a) The real Jeanne Harper was the wife of a coach-maker in Bettfield, and the woman who borrowed her name was actually called Dana Hesketh.

b) Arabella Coombs was far too self-impressed to ever dream of scoping out someone else's party.

c) Theresa was quite correct, the thief did not leave the salon with the box.

d) Bobby Vincent was always a little awkward around attractive women.

e) Iver was deeply relieved when Bobby returned to keep the thief busy, although he didn't show it.

f) Oswald Ware was genuinely flattered when Miss Miller described him as odd.

g) Mattie Vincent's design sensibilities leaned to the melodramatic, but she did have an exquisite sense of balance.

h) The box was not hidden in the salon.

i) The following week, Aubrey the cat recovered fully from his chest infection.

SOLUTIONS

LEVEL ONE

No.1 The Tailor. ....page 10

Daniel Hanson's shirt is green, and tattered muslin could quite feasibly have shed the bits of green thread found on the victim's clothes, particularly if he removed his jacket before the assault to avoid the possibility of getting blood on it. None of the other men questioned have anything that corresponds to any of the trace evidence. The gloves found with the body were eventually found to belong to Hanson's uncle, at which point Hanson confessed to the murder, and revealed where he'd stashed the items he'd killed the tailor for.

No.2 Rebecca ....page 14

If the house is exactly as the dead woman left it—with all the windows tightly closed—then how could she have jumped from one of them?

No.3 Introducing Mrs. Warren ....page 18

Bronze doesn't rust, so the smears on the air grille have to be dried blood. The grille is a great place to hide something fairly small temporarily, and its looseness suggests hasty fastening and unfastening. The thief accidentally broke the lamp while stashing stolen goods in the vent, cutting herself in the process. The only woman with noticeable wounds on her hands is Meagan.

The next day, as Emma expected, the girl snuck into the room to hide the watch left out in a room by Emma's boss, as witnessed by the hotel manager himself. The thief was passed to the police, and McGill gave Emma's firm a significant bonus for settling the matter so swiftly and quietly.

No.4 The Throttled Clerk ....page 21

The dead man has filthy shoes, but the floor he was found on is spotless. He must have been placed there after his death, which means that the killer knew where he lived. The murder was traced to a plot to rob the bank that Winton worked for, and the conspirators eventually confessed to tracking down the dead man, forcing information out of him, and then killing him to keep him quiet.

No.5 The Widower ....page 25

Lichtenberg figures—red, fern-like wounds—are caused by lightning strikes or similar point-sources of very strong electrical current. Imelda was found outside after a thunderstorm, and it was being out in the storm that killed her. She was struck whilst standing by the statue. The bolt discharged down her back, making her back muscles contract viciously so that her head smacked back into the statue, killing her.

No.6 Nail Polish. ....page 29

The old woman claims to have smelled gin on the breath of a maid she dislikes from down a hallway, but she isn't aware of the pervasive and distinctive smell of a particular dish. It seems unlikely, particularly when you factor in the old woman's bigotry and the maid's good record. Maureen took the old woman aside and after some stern questions, she admitted that she herself had taken the "scandalous" items from her great-niece's room, and as a two-for-one, attempted to use them to be rid of the maid she didn't like.

No.7 The Harkaway ....page 33

The apple core that the angry customer was pushing around was deeply tarnished with exposure to the air. That takes a significant period. The woman says she finished with her dessert and went to the bathroom, then came back and yelled immediately for Emma. Somewhere in that summary, there's half an hour of time unaccounted for.

It took a while, but they got the woman to admit that she was actually away from her table for a good twenty-five minutes, courtesy of some embarrassing constipation. The extended period of opportunity on the entry and exit list revealed the solo exit of a man who had entered some few minutes before, apparently as part of a group. The thief came back again two days later, and with Hal giving Emma an alert, he was caught in the act.

No.8 Bishop ....page 37

The damage to Walter's arm, a radiating break on his underarm, is a defensive wound, one you receive if you raise your arm to ward off an attack. Such damage is very unlikely to come from a fist. Bishop's account of events makes no allowance for his using weaponry on Walter, or in fact for any extended fighting. When Parnacki's team dug into the company business carefully, they discovered that there was no Danish deal, and Herr Nilaus did not, in fact, exist. Ian Bishop had been stealing money from the company for months. When Walter finally noticed and confronted him, his partner killed him.

No.9 Panhurst ....page 40

The village is pitch black, and Ania needs a flashlight to make her way back home, but Mrs. Colfer not only saw the intruder and where he went, but got a clear enough view to tell the hue of his dark shirt, and to identify the style of his footwear? It's highly implausible. When Ania spoke to the police again, they searched Mrs. Colfer's house thoroughly and found the stolen medicine chest, which she'd long coveted.

No.10 Pergamum ....page 44

Despite the impressive fight, the cause of death was a deep stab into the heart, from the back. This fits with the one piece of damage to Manby's office chair. In a brawl, there would be no reason for that particular chair to have been stabbed, given that it remains in its original position. If it had been part of the ruckus, it would have been disturbed. So the likelihood is that the murderer came up behind Manby sitting at his desk, and killed him with one well-placed blow. Like the dagger in the eye, the rest of the chaos is just window-dressing to confuse the matter. Thin daggers are often the preferred weapons of those with less physical strength, because a smaller blade increases the force of the stab, even though it requires greater precision.

Despite Parnacki's insight, the plausible candidates all had strong, corroborated alibis, and the murder was never officially solved.

No.11 Star House ....page 48

Regardless of the movements possibly observed by staff, the thief trampled a bed of purple flowers in the process of getting in to steal the parrot statuette. Barry has bits of purple flower on his trouser legs and shoes, marking him as the likely thief. When Miss Miller and Leona Whitten confronted him in front of the other men, he confessed to being smitten with the bird and taking it for his own.

No.12 The Fisherman ....page 53

It's afternoon, so Mason has been dead for at least eighteen hours, and his fish have been dead for longer than that. Dead fish start to become smelly in less than twelve hours, but the only scent at the scene is a faint trace of blood. The fish have to be significantly fresher than the evening before, and that makes Cox a liar. After some interrogation, Cox admitted to the murder. He was desperate for money, and owned more than twenty pieces of Mason's, as well as two more finished pieces he'd stolen. His hope had been that a murder would make the man's work shoot up in value.

No.13 Gas...page 57

It's clear that the evacuation sirens are a serious business, enough to kill people, and to leave dangerous situations unattended. The siren was not a planned drill. So why is Jared Alexander so insouciant? The thief, having triggered the evacuation, would know it's nothing to be worried about and, perhaps, would be overly keen to seem at his ease. Security staff forced the man's personal locker, and discovered the stolen item, and he was arrested a short time after.

No.14 Defenestration ....page 61

Berry's bad leg is well documented. It's not easy to get someone out of a window even if they're passive. It would be very hard for a man who needs a cane to forcibly defenestrate a struggling victim. Berry finally admitted that he had been bribed to draw police suspicion onto himself by the real murderer, a long-standing fraudster whom the victim had uncovered in the course of his work. Berry had been relying on his injury to get him off any murder charge, but was unprepared for the prospect of being arrested for conspiracy.

No.15 The Halcyon Rooms....................................page 66

The police have confiscated the cosmetics, but they have not taken the costume, and the facial prosthetic was late arriving from its manufacturer. When that was passed to the police for analysis, they discovered significant amounts of cyanide in the costume glue, particularly around its nostrils. The manufacturer reported that someone from the Halcyon Rooms had come to collect it, whilst David Knowles insisted it had been delivered. Lorna Avery was immediately ruled out as a suspect. The case rumbled on for months, eventually culminating in the arrest of one of Sally Wilde's former lovers.

No.16 The Gem Shop ....page 71

Mr. Baldwin was supposedly hit on the head and on the verge of passing out, in a dark room—but he somehow knows that the thief was using a sack made of silk? He has to be lying. In addition, if he had genuinely suffered head wounds violent enough to render him unconscious for several hours, he would be in the hospital, in a far more serious condition. Baldwin staged the break-in for the insurance payoff, and hoped to pin the guilt on one of his hapless employees.

No.17 Friday Night Special ....page 75

Toby Black is the murderer. In his testimony, he said that he saw the killer approach Knox from behind, and shoot him in the back. However, the note in Knox's breast pocket had been hit by the bullet, which was later removed from the body, so Knox must have been shot from the front. Black is lying to try to throw the police off the scent.

No.18 The Foreman Pieces...............................page 79

Stella clearly states that the newspaper reported five statuettes had been taken. The only way that Coombs could know that there were only three missing is if he were party to the theft.

No.19 The Miser ....page 83

The maid spread the news that Meyers was killed with a poker, but a weaponized poker is nearly always used as a bludgeoning weapon. Evan Patterson knows that Meyers was stabbed. The only way he could be aware of that detail is if he was the one who committed the crime.

No.20 Victor's Funeral ....page 87

Agatha's ignorance rests on her deafness, but she reacts to the gardener's shout at the same time as Miss Miller. If she can hear a man shout across a busy reception, she can definitely hear a gunshot in the next room—and quite possibly the argument that preceded it.

No.21 The Tip ....page 91

Books are numbered starting from the front side of their first loose page. Pages 69 and 70 are the front and back of the same piece of paper. Whatever the book was, it's impossible for anything to be inserted between those two pages.

No.22 The Narcissist ....page 95

Anthony Stewart knows that Pearce was working on a shipping manifest, despite arriving after the body had been found. Michael Solis attested that Pearce was private about his early-morning paperwork, and the body was slumped onto the desk, with blood over everything. The most likely way that Stewart could know what Pearce had been working on is that he had been the killer. After a short investigation, he confessed. Unable to tolerate Pearce's temper-tantrums and bullying any further, he had come in early and cut the man's throat.

No.23 Price's Mistake ....page 99

All the interviewees have solid alibis for the period after the talk, and none of them have alibis for the time beforehand. But the only person who knew about the change in the will before the meeting was Shane Massey. This means that no one else had a motive to kill Ben at the time when the poisoning took place, so he has to be the murderer. He had been expecting Ben's portion of the company, as per the existing will, but the thought that he would have to share control of the business with a cat charity was too much for him. Once he realized that Ben would not relent, he poisoned him with a slow-onset toxin and made sure he had a strong alibi for the rest of the evening, leaving the members of the family as apparently the only suspects.

No.24 Southwell Stowe ....page 103

At night in the country it's difficult to see anything outdoors, let alone from inside a lit room. It would have been very hard indeed for the maid to make out that much detail from that distance, particularly specific clothing. When the police arrived, they found Andrew Fonseca's goods at the bottom of the maid's drawer. She confessed shortly after.

No.25 Maynard's .... page 107

James was alone when the flowers arrived, and has seen no one but Tracey Kenyon and Miss Miller since. If Sue Terry has been in the main gallery all evening, how does she know anything about the flowers that were delivered? The manager agreed to discretely call police before the woman finished her evening's work, and the stolen purse was readily recovered.

No.26 Schaeffer and Sons.................................. page 112

Including Spagnuolo, the group of play-goers totals seven people. But sixty pence is not divisible by seven. He's lying.

No.27 The Phillips Suites .... page 117

Wooden dentures are not valuable. There's no useful reason to steal them. Unless, that is, you were bitten by them during a fight, and need to make sure that they cannot be matched to your wound. The police reluctantly agreed to search Edward Kendrick's home, where they found the stolen goods. He was duly arrested, convicted, and imprisoned.

No.28 Howard's End .... page 122

The bruise around the wound is a diamond shape with straight edges—the same as the unusual cross-guard on the hunting knife outside, set oddly amongst the woodworking tools.

No.29 Cartwright .... page 126

Alan, Mrs. Abouelela's son, blamed his wet sleeve on a shower whilst out walking, but the sky had been blue all day. When his mother interrogated him, forcefully, he admitted to the thefts. He'd been having money problems, and had been too frightened of her to admit it.

No.30 The Boat .... page 130

If the two men were on a boat being tossed back and forth during a storm, how could they have been playing a board game?

No.31 The Warehouse .... page 134

In the warehouse, it was 9.05 am before Emma had finished cleaning the packing machine. A minute or two later, in the manager's office, 2.40 am is said to be more than six hours earlier. The clocks don't agree, and the culprit would only have had access to the warehouse clock. So the warehouse clock—and the foreman's reported times—are half an hour fast. The thief must be the man who went on break at what the foreman thought was 3 am.

No.32 The Banker .... page 138

Johnson's wife had only been in hospital for a day or so before the murder, so elaborate planning is unlikely. Of the three men, only Matt has feet small enough to fit into a size eight boot. Evidence later discovered at his home corroborated Parnacki's suspicion. The three brothers maintained their mutual alibi throughout the trial, and the victim's famed manner provided sufficient doubt to secure a verdict of not guilty.

No.33 Hatchards .... page 141

The company logo is three concentric rings with a line straight through the middle. The flag is identical either way up. Andrew MacLean-Finney is lying, and clumsily. Although he protested innocence on the premises, in police questioning he confessed to taking the documents, and revealed their location. His plan had been to use them as the basis of a new competing company.

No.34 Get Carter .... page 146

Your trousers—or anything else fastened around your waist—sit higher on your legs when you are sitting than they do when you are standing or lying down. If Carter had been stabbed while he was sitting down, the hole in the fabric would not be perfectly aligned with the hole in his leg. The scene had to be staged, which means that he was murdered. Eventually, after a scandalous investigation, one of Knight's directors was proved to have ties to organized crime, and Carter to have been one of his minions. When Emma started getting close, the man had him murdered.

No.35 The Mask .... page 149

When Miss Miller was collecting her toiletries in the morning, there was a shard of glass in her bag. Since a piece of delicate crystal is missing, it seems distinctly possible that it was broken and the shard was from that. The shard must must have fallen in while the bag was open. That rules out the maid who aired the room, the coachman who brought the bag up, and the extra help who brought the bag back down. Amelia later let her know that the maid who'd been making the bed in the evening had accidentally bumped the case, and the mask had fallen and shattered. She'd been scared to admit to it, and had hoped that its fate might be left uncertain by the large influx of guests and assistant staff for the dinner party. The girl had only been with Amelia for a few months, and was duly cautioned to be honest about accidents.

No.36 McDowell .... page 152

The report from the scene says that the victim is covered in blood, including his hands and head, but there is no sign of it on the telephone. It's very unlikely McDowell would have been able to make the call that the station received without smearing the telephone as well. Williams' alibi is strong, but it relies entirely on the time estimate from the call being accurate. After the murder weapon was found hastily buried in Williams' garden, he admitted to jealously killing McDowell, staging the murder scene, and then placing the telephone call himself to provide him with an alibi.

No.37 Riverside .... page 155

The kitchen is full of sinks and basins. Why is a kitchen maid crossing the house to wash her hands? It suggests some sort of deception is in place.

When Sophia and Miss Miller retraced the girl's steps, they found an ivory comb carefully stashed inside a large water carafe. The girl confessed readily rather than be turned over to the police.

No.38 The Industrial Museum .... page 159

When the tour group went in, they had to move very slowly to make allowance for the one-legged old man. On their way out, though, they are all running—his disability has to be at least partially feigned, and that, combined with the convenient hasty exit due to a sudden fire bell, makes it very unlikely that he's simply engaged in some very odd prank.

Drabwell's security apprehended him, and discovered that he was significantly less old than he appeared, and bipedal besides. Stolen artefacts were retrieved from the false peg leg, and after an investigation, the man was charged, along with several accomplices: the overdressed young woman, the two suited men, and two lower-level members of the museum staff.

No.39 Pelton Street .... page 163

There are delivery invoices in the kitchen that include milk. The milkman has just delivered to the area. But there are no bottles, empty or full, outside the house. That would make sense if Mrs. Ellis had warned him she'd be away, but if not, then her regular standing order would have been delivered. If milk had been left untouched, the milkman might have replaced old bottles with fresh, or added new bottles to the pile, but he wouldn't have just taken the delivery away. A nearby resident might have pinched them possibly, but then the milkman would have delivered more as usual. The only simple explanation is that he knew not to deliver.

When Parnacki caught up with the milkman, he said that five mornings ago, he'd been delivering as usual when a man claiming to be the woman's son left the house. This fellow told the milkman that Mrs. Ellis was leaving for a few weeks, and would give him a note when she returned. The man was eventually identified, with the milkman's help, as the illicit lover of a woman over the road, another man's wife. The old woman had seen them sneaking around, and when she smugly informed the wife that she was going to tell the husband, the lover came over before she could do so, and throttled her to death.

LEVEL TWO

No. 40 The Pastoral Carving .... page 168

The Harlequinade is a theatrical slapstick farce performed primarily in mime, set to music. Most of the characters—including Pantaloon—wear specific traditional costumes and masks to identify them to the audience. George Wallis led his understudy to believe that he had an assignation with the playhouse director's daughter, and the man agreed to fill in for him secretly in the first act, in return for a small bribe. In full costume, with no lines to speak, the man was effectively indistinguishable, even to the other cast. They swapped back over in Wallis's dressing room for the second act. Wallis would not normally have resorted to crime, but he was disliked, and his father would never have handed over the money required for the *netsuke*.

Following Miss Miller's suggestion of how Wallis might have been responsible, Mendez sent an agent to Wallis's rooms in search of the piece. It was retrieved, and Wallis was informed that he was blacklisted, and warned quite pointedly about the perils of any further transgressions.

No. 41 Horton & Creak .... page 178

The coffee is the key. Coggen's office and chair are spotless, but the body had significant coffee stains. There are also coffee stains in Wilkins' office, on his chair and his paperwork. We know Wilkins' office is untidy right now, but he himself is fastidious, and his office is usually ordely. So why would the seat of his chair be stained?

No one had a motive to kill Edwin Coggen, because he was not the intended victim. He was in Wilkins' office, helping solve his logistical problem. The killer—the husband of the woman Wilkins was having an affair with—came to leave a warning letter, but when he saw the man there working, he snapped and killed him. Too late, he realized that he'd murdered Edwin Coggen. To avoid suspicion, he waited until the company was quiet, then moved Coggen back to his own office and fled.

Once Parnacki realized that Coggen had been a mistaken death, affairs progressed smoothly. Wilkins realized the danger he was in when this was suggested to him, and identified his current lover. The husband, already guilt-wracked, confessed quickly. Wilkins reluctantly resigned shortly afterwards, to be replaced by James Weedon.

No.42 The Baxter Affair...................................page 187

Emma's question was "What have you done with your sister, Damian?"

The correct *Ave Maria* is "Hail Mary, full of grace, the Lord is with thee. Blessed art thou amongst women, and blessed is the fruit of thy womb, Jesus. Holy Mary, Mother of God, pray for us sinners, now and at the hour of our death. Amen." There is no chance whatsoever that a long-serving nun would forget to include Jesus in any prayer, let alone such a common one.

Damian considered trying to bolt, but Bridget Radcliffe had already leapt up to stand in front of the door, and he folded. He was desperate for money, and after his uncle refused once again to help, Damian killed him with the idea of getting his sister to aid him from her inheritance instead. He met her in the city, and when she wouldn't agree to give him the money, he subdued her and left her restrained in a room in a cheap flophouse. Two weeks after his arrest, he was murdered in his jail cell by an agent working for his creditors.

No.43 The Man in the Barrel............................page 195

Chase Costello was murdered by his brother, Roman, but the plan was Dessie's. When Chase realized that his business was going under, he made sure his life insurance policy was up to date and cooked up a scheme with his wife. Chase pretended to vanish, and went to hide out in the cabin on the land he had just purchased. He then found a hobo of a similar build and age, and killed him. He made sure the body was unrecognizable, dressed it in some of his spare clothes and dumped it in the river.

The idea was that after Chase had been missing for a few days, Dessie would identify the body as his, claim on the life insurance, and then they'd start a new life together elsewhere.

But Dessie saw the future differently. She and Roman had fallen in love, and Chase's plan provided a perfect opportunity for them to be together. She persuaded Chase to wait a bit longer while she made sure she was beyond suspicion before going to visit her family. Then Roman pretended to go hunting, and instead went to Chase's cabin, spent some time lulling Chase into a false sense of security, and killed him. He then dumped the body in a barrel at the docks to mislead the police into concentrating on the involvement of organized crime. Roman and Dessie also agreed to make people think she had been having an affair with Aristos, to muddy the waters further.

Roman was eventually convicted of murder, and Dessie of conspiracy. The one silver lining from the whole sad episode was that it brought Oscar and Aristos back together, leading to an enduring friendship.

No. 44 The Eye of Fire......................................page 203

The thief is the cook's assistant, and it's her height that gave her away. Since Miss Miller never got a good look at the blonde woman's face, she did not note that the woman had androgynous, unmemorable features. Her vivid lipstick and clouds of hair ensured that most other people didn't notice either.

As soon as the lights went out, the thief dashed to the stage, wiping off her lipstick on her sleeve. She dropped the gem into the cook's hat she had in her handbag. It was already prepared with a small amount of fake black hair visible at both front and back. She pulled on the hat and jumped down from the stage to the planter where she had stashed the jacket and trousers. Having pulled the cook's outfit on over her dress, she retrieved her flat shoes from her handbag, then put the wig and heels in the handbag, dumped it, slipped into the shoes, and made for the door. But as soon as the lights came on, the thief realized she was in trouble. She stood back against the wall and tried to look like a real cook's assistant.

Having noticed earlier that the turquoise-clad woman's heels were 3in high, and her height in them was 6ft, Miss Miller had already pegged her real height at 5ft 9in—tall for a woman, but not spectacularly so. As soon as she began to suspect the thief was still in the room after the lights had returned, Miss Miller started examining heights. Reasonably confident in her assumptions that both the thief was still there and that she wouldn't be sitting down, she checked out all the people standing up. Only the cook's assistant was the right height to be the missing woman.

No.45 The Grand Hotel ....page 211

Damian Edwards is the murderer, and his tie was the main thing that gave him away.

Having heard that Smallwood was in the hotel, Edwards decided to seize the opportunity to avenge his older brother, who died while working for Smallwood. He gained access to the room by pretending to deliver a bottle of complimentary champagne. When he got inside, Edwards quickly took off his jacket and stabbed Smallwood with the scissors he had brought along for that purpose.

Once the man was dead, Edwards realized that his own shirt and tie were covered in blood. He removed them and wiped himself off, throwing the bloody stuff onto the blazing fire. Then he hunted through the man's cases for replacements. He found a white shirt easily, but a black tie was the best he could do. Then he went to call the manager, knowing that if he spoke to the supervisor before everything was thrown into chaos, she would be likely to notice his tie was wrong.

The other major mistake Edwards made was to describe the door being opened by his invented murderer upon exiting—the door handle would have had bloody handprints on it if he'd been telling the truth. Also bear in mind that there's no real reason for Edwards to have known the identity of the dead man, and that it's quite unlikely that he would be tasked with checking a fruit bowl. That would be part of the maid's job when the room was being made up for the day, rather than an errand handed out at random in the afternoon.

No.46 The Twin page 220

Martin Eagleton is extremely careful throughout to refer to his client. Although Jeff Sparks is indeed his client, so is Jerrod Sparks—and their *other* brother, Joe Sparks. The three are identical triplets, and Joe's existence is kept a guarded secret. It was Joe and Jerrod who were holding court at the restaurant while Jeff led the raid on Garland's Fine Jewels. When Eagleton refers to his client, he is actually talking about Joe. When Parnacki suggested a third brother, Eagleton and Sparks clammed up completely. The case took a long time to build, and almost as long in trial, but eventually all three Sparks brothers were convicted and imprisoned.

No.47 Matilda's Birthday page 229

The thief took the balloons from one end of the flower basket and tied the empty box to them, then released them on the balcony. Miss Miller actually saw the balloons as they floated away, but they were too distant at that point for the box to be visible. When the police arrived, the thief was still being shown around by Bobby Vincent, who kept her interested with promises of showing her some more easily filched valuables in a little while. She was arrested, and when the police got her back to the station, the diamond choker was found on her person.

Printed in the United States
by Baker & Taylor Publisher Services